Cast Your Nets Wide:

How To Approach, Meet, and Have Any Woman You Desire

Joe Alpha Special Edition

By

Joe Alpha

Joe Alpha Press

joealpha.com

Copyright Notice

All rights are reserved.

No part of this publication may be reproduced, stored in a retrieval system or transmitted in any form or by any means, electronic, mechanical, photocopying, recording or otherwise, without prior permission.

Medical Disclaimer

Information contained in this book is intended as an educational aid only. No information contained in this book should be construed as medical or psychological advice or diagnosis. Readers should consult appropriate health professionals on any matter relating to their health and well-being.

Copyright © 2011, 2012 Joe Alpha Factor

ISBN: 0615612504
ISBN-13: 978-0615612508

THANKS

Special thanks to Natalie Howard our female model for the photographs. For all your graphic design needs, visit Natalie, the Blond Bombshell Geek, at nhoward.com.

CONTENTS

Part I: Human Nature	8
Chapter 1: It's Time to Approach...But Not Just Yet	9
Chapter 2: Important Terminology and Concepts	13
Chapter 3: What Men and Women Want	20
Chapter 4: Your Inner Disposition/Inner Game	33
Part II: Overcoming Approach Anxiety	52
Chapter 5: Approach Anxiety	53
Chapter 6: Death by Rejection?	59
Chapter 7: Techniques to Reduce Approach Anxiety	65
Chapter 8: Final Thoughts on Approach Anxiety	74
Part III: The Body Language of Attraction	77
Chapter 9: The Importance of Body Language	78
Chapter 10: How Body Language Works	82
Chapter 11: Reading the Room	88
Chapter 12: Knowing The Easiest Girls To Approach	106
Chapter 13: Physical Signs She Is Attracted To You	118
Chapter 14: Your Attractive Body Language	125
Chapter 15: Final Thoughts on Body Language	147
Part IV: What to Say and How to Say It	149
Chapter 16: Environments	150
Chapter 17: Talk Dammit!	158
Chapter 18: Demonstrate Value	171
Chapter 19: Building Rapport and Making Connections	187
Chapter 20: Closing and Follow-Up	202
Chapter 21: Building a Relationship and Sex	215
Chapter 22: Attitude	227
Chapter 23: AMOG: The Tribal Leader	245
Chapter 24: Conclusion	258
Bonus 1: Social Media Mistakes You Are Making	263
Bonus 2: Six Quick Tips To Meet Women At The Gym	270
Bibliography and Suggested Reading	275

THE ALPHA MALE

An Alpha Male is the leader of men. He is charismatic. He thinks abundantly, therefore he is generous. Women love him, men want to be him. He is focused on what he is doing, and he does the right thing despite the outcome. He is detached and flexible. He takes care of others, especially friends and family. He is empathetic, and has instant rapport with whomever he meets. He is confident, and not arrogant. He knows and communicates his high value to others. The Alpha Male creates his own reality, and he does not borrow it from others. He is completely, irresistibly, and infinitely abundantly attractive in all areas of his life. He operates from a position of "power," not "force."

At The Joe Alpha Factor, we are dedicated to helping men and women reframe their reality so that they can attract into their lives health, wealth, money, and friends. Note that we capitalize the term "Alpha Male" throughout this book because we are referring to our unique understanding of the term.

Please enjoy this book. It is fun, informative, and to the point. We promise there is no filler here, just high quality, concise and practical advice you can use - right now!

Part I: Human Nature

Chapter One: It's Time to Approach..... But Not Just Yet...

So, you want to meet women! Great! That means you are a normal, red blooded human being who wants to secure his place in immortality! We are going to teach you how to do just that in this book.

In gathering the research, through personal experience with women, as well as research that includes neurology, psychology, and philosophy, in addition to the social dynamics, we have realized just how vast the subject of relationships, and the nuances related to them, can be! So, let me provide a disclaimer, which is that this book is not exhaustive of human nature in general, although it specifically covers the aspects of meeting, building, and maintaining relationships with women.

As of the publication of this particular guide to approaching women, we are still in the process of doing our research, both personally, with our own experiences with women, as well as looking into the mainstream, and even fringes, of the study of human nature. That means more is to be discovered and more is to be written on the subject.

In this book, we will explore very specific aspects of human nature, especially in regard to how to overcome your fear (approach anxiety) as well as how to read certain aspects of women and how to project yourself physically, which is known as body language, and how to form and maintain relationships with members of the opposite sex. This book therefore cannot possibly delve into all the profound aspects of approaching and dealing with women, so we will limit ourselves to some ways to rethink your approach, some methods on how to approach, as well as the most important thing, how to get her number so you can talk to her again and deepen the relationship.

This book, therefore, will focus most of all on the approach, and what to do and what to say so that you will have a better chance of continuing the conversation with someone you might find attractive and interesting. It will also be an exploration of human nature - the most fascinating subject in the world!

The funny thing about human nature is that it is an exact science, while at the same time a guessing game. Think of poker. Ever watch poker on television? It is a mix of knowing the facts about the cards, the deck, the probability of this or that card, but it is also about reading the subjective parts of the game, such as the tells the opponent gives, which include expressions, tonality, and body language. It is a game.

Well, start thinking that way about human nature. It is a game. Some people know the rules of the game, and others don't. The people that know the rules of the game, both the objective and subjective aspects, are the most successful at it. That doesn't just go for women either. This is a general truth that applies to the game of life, whether you are dealing with business, like Donald Trump, politics, like Bill Clinton, or religion - don't think the Pope doesn't know the rules of the game of life. These are, by the way, a list of some of my favorite Alpha Males.

Pick-Up Artists?!

Before we begin to understand how to approach women, I think we should address a few important points.

First, if you have read any of our other books, you know that The Joe Alpha Factor does not claim to create pick-up artists. Pick-up artists, or PUAs as they will be referred to in this book, can generally be thought of as men who use particular methods of seduction to get women into bed. PUAs, and their techniques, are generally not about deepening relationships with women. It is about seduction.

At The Joe Alpha Factor, however, we are about creating Alpha Males: leaders of men and protectors of their tribe, who understand their responsibility in the community, and leave people better than they found them.

So sit back, relax, and enjoy learning about humanity. This will help you, not only in your interactions with women you are romantically interested in, but people in general. Also, check back with us at www.joealpha.com as we explore other specific aspects of humanity that will help you win the game of life (The real version, not the Milton Bradley version you played as a kid)!

Chapter Two: Important Terminology and Concepts

Now that we have set some of the frame (more on that later), we need to introduce some terms that we will be using regularly, so we can be on the same page.

The Alpha Male

The first important concept is one that is central to The Joe Alpha Factor, and that is the Alpha Male. Creating true Alpha Males is what we do. An Alpha Male is a guy who, if he is not in control of his environment, is a heavy influence on it. He is a guy who is amicable, but confident. He does what is right even if it isn't popular. His confidence, which is a mix of the understanding of his deep value, as well as his fearlessness, is what is most attractive about him. He may not be the fastest, funniest, or even smartest guy in the room, but he influences and directs the fastest, funniest, and smartest guy in the room. That makes him the leader of them all, and he puts their abilities at his disposal.

The Alpha Male has learned social skills that allow him to make deep connections with people very quickly. He understands the value of emotion, but at the same time, he is detached from it, so that he can always make the next right step or move. Women love him, and men want to be him, or at the very least, stand in his aura. They WANT to follow the Alpha Male. Finally, the Alpha Male never wants for anything, as he attracts wealth at the same time he attracts people. In fact, he is generous before he takes, and always sees the abundance in the world, especially when others see scarcity.

An Alpha has the common good of the tribe in mind, and is not simply in it for himself.

This book, as our other books, tries to capture the Alpha Male frame of mind, so that you can too! Alpha Males are not born; they are made. That means there is hope for you as well, even if you don't think of yourself as an Alpha Male.

The Beta and The Gamma Male: Two Sides of the Same Coin

The term Alpha and Beta Males are based on studies of primates and other animals, and are applied to humans, especially males, as well. In the animal kingdom, the Alpha is the leader of the troupe, or in the case of dogs, the pack. He is the strongest and best, and everyone else is considered a Beta Male.

When it comes to humans, however, the term Beta Male takes on a negative connotation. Yes, like in the animal kingdom, the Beta is a follower, but there is a reason he is a follower and not a leader. That reason is that he lacks the confidence that the Alpha has. The Beta Male does not understand his own value, is not assertive or straight forward, and "plays it safe" in the shadow of the Alpha Male. The Beta Male sees things from a position of scarcity, and therefore waits, like the vulture, to get the leftovers. The Beta Male is passive-aggressive in this regard, and will try to bribe people into liking him through favors, compliments, and butt-kissing. People tolerate most Betas because they are essentially harmless, and even helpful, because they are happy to do everyone's bidding, for a few scraps from the table.

Women generally are repulsed by Beta Males. Again, a Beta Male is good "friend" material. He is someone that will help them move their stuff into their new apartment. He is pleasant to talk to, because the Beta listens to her endless problems in the hope that if he listens long enough, she might like him in romantically. It never happens. Poor guy. We feel sorry for him, because he is so fragile inside that he never takes the risks necessary to get what he really wants, or what he thinks he wants.

He is a "nice guy."

Finally, the Beta Male is in it for one person: himself. He follows, he bribes, he whines, and he pulls weird passive-aggressive actions because he is only looking out for himself. No woman is attracted to that. Ever.

The Gamma Male on the other hand is a designation unique to The Joe Alpha Factor. We coined it from the Greek word for "ass" which starts with the Greek letter "gamma." The Gamma Male seems to be the opposite of the Beta Male. If the Beta Male is passive-aggressive, then the Gamma Male is aggressive. The passive-aggressive Beta Male appears nice and passive, but is really plotting behind your back to do whatever it takes to serve his own needs. The aggressive Gamma Male is the "jerk" or the "asshole." This is the high school jerk that was fond of stuffing Beta Males in lockers, and forcing their heads down toilets. This guy often has a lot of tribal tattoos, wears Ed Hardy shirts, and beats up his girlfriend or wife, although there are many Gamma Males in business that look quite presentable. A Gamma is an jerk in life, and on the field. Some of them are pretty smart, and they use this to bulldoze their way through life. He is the guy that always wants to fight, and he usually throws the first punch. He tries to be the Alpha Male by brute force, whereas the Alpha leads by power, through his confidence and charisma.

Gammas are in it for themselves, and will hurt people to get their way. And when they do get their way, they will drop the people that they used to get it. They are, in essence, bullies.

Pretty much every woman has dated a Gamma or two (or three or four), because women love Gammas. First, it is easy to confuse their aggressiveness with the assertiveness and confidence of the Alpha Male. Both, on the surface, appear to have similar qualities, but the similarities are only skin deep. The aggressive Gamma responds to others with anger and physical threats, while the assertive Alpha responds with confidence and poise. The Alpha provides and protects, whereas the Gamma just takes and uses.

Many women have stories to tell about their times with Gamma Males, and the stories usually involve heartache and bankruptcy.

Why do we say that the Beta and the Gamma are really just two sides of the same coin? While it seems that they act very differently, they are actually very much the same at the core. The core is what matters. In the above paragraph, I mentioned that Alphas and Gammas look alike on the surface, but those similarities are usually only skin deep. The opposite is true for Gammas and Betas. They seem very different on the surface, but at the core they are the same guy.

Both the Gamma and the Beta are insecure. They do not understand their worth, and therefore they do not understand the worth of others. As mentioned earlier, both are aggressive in their own way, and both are self-centered narcissists that will use people for their own ends. Psychologist Dr. David Lieberman believes that there is a difference between aggressiveness and assertiveness, and the difference is an understanding of their own value. A person that understands his value will have no need to be aggressive, but will have the confidence to be assertive. Assertive is good, aggressive is bad.

I highly recommend the excellent book <u>Power Vs. Force</u> by Dr. David Hawkins. "Force," a negative term in that book, is when someone uses negative means, like pride, guilt, fear, or shame, to achieve an end. These "forceful" strategies are the hallmarks of the

Beta and the Gamma. "Power," a powerful means to an end, is the hallmark of the Alpha Male. He uses charisma, hope, courage, etc. to achieve his ends. Yes, it take a little more investment of time and energy to be "powerful," but the long term effects speak for themselves. And a high energy, powerful Alpha will *always* beat out low energy, forceful Betas and Gammas in any situation.

Attraction: It is the Law

While there are some other distinctions, we will be using these terms to discuss the right and wrong ways to deal with women. This brings us to an important, if not *the* most important, concept in this book: Attractiveness.

The Alpha Male is attractive. We have said this a few times before. He is powerful, attentive, and mindful. He is a leader and looks out for the weak. These characteristics are super attractive to women, and hell, they are attractive to anyone! This book is about approaching women, but pretty much everything that we write about at The Joe Alpha Factor is about being attractive. We are not just concerned with being attractive to women: the Alpha Male attracts anything and everything to himself. He doesn't have to force anything from anybody. His power comes from his understanding of his value, and his ability to communicate that value to others. If he doesn't believe that he has value, and if he doesn't believe that he will be attractive, then neither will the people he interacts with.

So, do yourself a favor. If you feel insecure, start shifting your focus, now, to the things that are valuable about you. Maybe you aren't the best looking dude in the room, but neither was Abraham Lincoln. Maybe you aren't eloquent, but neither was Caesar. Maybe you have some disability. So did Einstein. All of these guys were Alpha Males though, because they knew the things that gave them high value, and were able to communicate that to the people around them. That means you can too.

Second, start seeing the value in others. People want to be treated like they matter, and they will do all sorts of crazy crap to feel validated. Do it for them and you will have followers for life.

Being attractive is a *choice*. It is the choice of where you put your focus, and if you focus on being excellent, you will also be attractive. People will flock to you, and you will have so much abundance of everything in your life, you won't know what to do with all of the people, wealth, and opportunities that this life has to offer to you!

Women can easily spot a man that believes in his worth from a mile away. She can also tell a guy who doesn't. Which one do you think she wants to be with? Yeah, you know the answer! But is that guy you?

Chapter Three: What Men and Women Want

We Homo Sapiens have been around for about 300,000 years or so, in our current form. 300,001 years ago, we were something a little different. We were humanoid, but not quite humans, something a little closer to an ape than a full-fledged human being. We didn't think the same way, conceptualize the same way, wonder about the future the same way, or remember the past the same way as we do now, yet whatever that creature was, was probably more like us than different. It took millions of years to evolve into our present form, with our well-formed, complex brains, and a wonderful neocortex that allows us to do all sorts of advanced tasks, from designing buildings to reading this book!

That neocortex part of the brain is relatively new. In terms of our evolution, it is only 300,000 years old, but its development separated us from other primate ancestors. I personally think it is a work in process, and if you look at the evolutionary leap we have made in science and technology in the last 150 years or so, you can see that evolution is still alive and well!

When you read the part of this book on the Body Language of Attraction, you will know that we have two parts to our brain, the "back of the brain," known as the "reptilian brain," that we share with all mammals, as well as other non-mammal vertebrates, and that neocortex, which sits just behind and slightly above your eyes.

Our brain has two operating systems: the "back of the brain," which runs like Windows, and the neocortex, which runs like a Mac. The two are both important for the whole brain to work, and sometimes they happily work together, but often they are at war, struggling to see which runs the show.

The back of the brain does all sorts of fun operations, like processing visual information, connecting concepts to words, reacting to danger or pleasure, and keeping our bodily functions operating. It is also responsible for determining what we are attracted to. That "back of the brain," is *ooooold* technology. It is more like Windows 3.1 than Windows 7. Well, actually, it is more like DOS. While it is more complex than, let's say, a monkey or cat, it still performs the same basic tasks. Those tasks have been hard wired into us for hundreds of thousands, and we can safely say, *millions* of years, through evolution. Remember, my dear friends, just "yesterday" we were building pyramids. That was 6000 years ago. Humans have been around for more than 300,000 years!

The back of the brain goes back even further, of course, and helps us navigate easily through life. A lot of what we do is the result of the back of the brain's "automatic pilot." That includes what we are attracted to.

That is not to say that the front of the brain, the "thinking brain," doesn't have a lot of influence. It essentially has the great ability to direct our attention toward or away from things, which the back of the brain then reacts to. It can override the automatic programming that is hard wired into us through years of evolution. Biology is not destiny. Not Necessarily. However, to override the back of the brain requires attention and focus, which a lot of people do not consciously utilize. That means that a lot of people are guided by old fashioned, biological urges. If you know about these urges, it will help you to influence whatever situation you might find yourselves in.

We will dive deeper into these two "operating systems" later in the book.

That being said, what is the back of the brain wired for? Two things: survival, and procreation. That is what all lower animals are wired for, isn't it? Even as humans, we are the way we are today because early humans and human ancestors with the most advanced brains survived more easily, and could pass their genes to the next generations. It is an issue of survival of the fittest in the truest sense. Think about horse breeders: they pick the horses with the best traits, and they breed them to make a superhorse (Although it is hard to get the tights and the cape on the Superhorse!). Well, nature does the same thing through a natural process. Therefore nature favors the survivors, and lets them breed more often. So, everything in the back of our brains really comes down to survival and procreation.

Every human interaction is based, somehow, on these two principles. The hunter in the forest is hunting in order to survive. The businessman, on the lookout for the next deal, is ultimately doing it to survive. The football player, trying to make the touchdown, is trying to help his "tribe" survive and go to the championship. As an aside, that is why we organize ourselves into tribes, so that we can aid each other in surviving and procreation. These survival instincts are utilized in a more complex way by the "thinking" brain, the neocortex, I have been mentioning.

So when it comes to romantic relationships, we have to understand that survival and procreation are the basis of human interaction and activity. Before we move on, however, we can see how even these can be overridden by the "thinking brain" for the common good, such as when a soldier dives on a grenade to save his platoon. That is Alpha Male action at its finest, by the way.

Let's hope you don't have to dive on any grenades! Even if you do get a few "bullet holes," the chapter on overcoming Approach Anxiety will help you to deal with rejection, and even embrace it.

This survival/procreative instinct manifests itself differently in men than it does in women. Because a lot of our activity is hard wired into us, it is important to understand human nature to deal with it properly. The nice thing is that with this guide, we are teaching you how to better utilize your thinking brain to better deal with the "back of the brain" of the people you will meet!

Males: Hunting for Immortality

Males manifest their survival and procreative wiring in a direct way. Men are wired to be direct, to face danger head on. That is why Beta Males are so repulsive: they are passive in their dealing with reality. Men have evolved, therefore, to be hunters, to go out into the forest, to look for game, and to kill it. You can't be a pansy when you are chasing down a saber tooth tiger or a mammoth. Being timid means that you will be cut into many pieces or stomped to death. When we encounter Alpha Males, we know that they will help us survive, lead us on successful "hunts" (even in the modern sense I outlined above), and so we want to follow them, because we know they have the survival of the whole tribe in mind.

In this sense, Alpha Males, both now and in human history, even among pre-human primates, have been more likely to procreate than Betas (we will talk about Gammas in a minute). When a woman looks at a Beta Male, she does not see someone who will help her survive anything. He is passive, and a follower, and in the jungle, passivity in a male means death.

The Alpha Male excels at survival, so he not only survives on his own, he helps others survive. So, he is more likely to reproduce and procreate, passing his superior genes on to the next generation.

Gamma Males are a different story. They too are wired for survival and procreation, but they focus entirely on their own survival. While they mimic some Alpha Male traits, because aggressiveness resembles assertiveness, Alphas and Gammas are very different. Since those two traits can be confused, Gamma Males successfully attract women, because aggressiveness is a trait that could aid in survival in the forest. The down side is that if presented between protecting himself, or his mate and his children, his choice is clear. He will always sacrifice others, even his relatives, in favor of himself. In the end, he does not get to pass down his genes as much, since he does not protect his offspring. In modern times, the survival advantage has shifted to Beta Males, especially in a monogamous system such as ours. Alpha Males only get one woman, and the rest are stuck with Beta Males. Beta Males have more advantage today than they have had throughout any time in human history, however the Alpha will always have the ultimate advantage.

The Alpha Male has more opportunities to reproduce in nature, because his ability to lead, provide, protect, and aid in survival is attractive to women, as well as to his Beta Males. The Alpha gets more reproductive chances because the Betas will never be able to attract as he can, and are likely to let him reproduce first and most often. Further, before modern times, and even into modern times, societies were polygamists, which meant that the Alpha Male would pass on his genes through several women, leaving the genetically weaker Betas to die without offspring.

In this sense, the Alpha is immortal, since he is the one who gets to live forever through his progeny. His ability to survive, provide, and protect others in his tribe, also gives him the right and the ability to live forever in his offspring. The Beta simply dies, and his lineage, or lack thereof, with him.

Since every Alpha Male needs a woman to reproduce with, what type of woman attracts the Alpha? Well, we can say this about men in general, even the Betas and Gammas: it is a woman's reproductive ability. Men want women that can provide them with healthy offspring. Healthy, fertile women. Don't believe me? (I know you do, though) Look at all the fertility cults and rituals that have been a part of universal human cultural experience. Every religion has it, be it the 72 virgins in the afterlife for Muslims (an expression of polygamy), the giant candle going into the baptismal font of the Catholics (a clear sign of sexuality), or even the purity laws of the Jews. All religions have some procreative aspect that is deeply embedded into their rituals and beliefs.

Men are attracted to women that are able to produce healthy babies, and keep them alive, basically, women that effectively survive and procreate. That means that men are attracted to traits like big boobs, long hair, and a .7 waist-to-hip ratio (i.e. a woman's waste is 70% the size of her hips), which is optimal for reproduction. This is why women wear tight clothes and make-up, and push up their boobs with bras and tight shirts. They are advertising their strong reproductive abilities!

So, the pressure is on women to be as physically attractive as possible. In some sense, women have the advantage when they are younger and fit. They have the ability to select the good men and weed out the bad, but this power begins to fade as they get older, and they begin to lose their reproductive abilities, or at least the signs of their reproductive abilities. This is why a lot of men go through a "mid-life crisis" by the way.

What?! Yea, think about it. Men can reproduce their whole lives, and do, which means that they always have the drive to procreate. Women get to a point where they can't, which is usually anywhere from their mid to late forties into their fifties. When do men have their "crisis?" The answer is, when their wives stop being fertile! They buy a new car, lose twenty pounds, and start becoming interested in pretty young girls in their twenties that are, you guessed it, fertile! Amazing huh? You cannot deny human nature. However, we do understand that there is free will, and biology is not destiny.

Males, therefore are hunters in two regards. In one way, they hunt for food, or in modern times, opportunities to physically survive and make money. In a second sense, they hunt for immortality through reproduction. Therefore, they are going to be attracted to women that have the signs of youth, health, and reproductive ability, and more important, women that have signs of availability. The most attractive female trait, at least to a man, is availability. We cover why that is in the Body Language of Attraction guide.

Women: Safety and Security, Provide and Protect

So what is it that women want? What type of man are they attracted to? Well, their "reptilian" brains are wired the same as everyone else: survival and procreation. But women have a very different nature than men, which means that their survival and procreative wiring manifests itself differently. Again, as a reminder, we are talking about ancient brain programming from hundreds of thousands, if not millions of years of evolution. Our programming hasn't changed that much in the last fifty years, and people still are wired to respond to the things we are talking about.

Women, by nature, tend to be smaller, slower, and weaker than men. This means that the way they interact with their environment is much more passive. Women simply can't meet the dangers of the jungle in a direct way as a male can. In the forest, they need to be protected, especially if they are pregnant or raising children. Raising children is particularly important for humans, because human offspring are not capable of doing anything for themselves for many years! More than ten and up to twenty! By the way, it is the long rearing process that helped evolve the neocortex, or the "thinking brain," that we mentioned before.

So, survival for a woman, again generally speaking, and her offspring, requires someone who can provide and protect her. If a pregnant female human, or a female with children in her care, is left alone in the forest without her protector, her chance of survival plummets, as do the children's.

Also, it is true is that eggs are much more valuable than sperm. Think about it this way: a woman produces one egg a month and her reproductive window is just a few days. So, if she does get pregnant, the maximum number of babies she can have in a year is one (discounting things like twins etc.). In comparison, a male produces millions of sperm a day, and can have as many babies as there are willing and fertile partners. Speaking in terms of survival, sperm, and males, are expendable, and are not as "valuable" as women and their eggs.

So a woman must be *very* careful what she does with her limited resources. She can't just throw eggs around the way. The male is just trying to get as many women pregnant as possible, to spread his genetic material as far and wide as he can. He can afford to be reckless, since he has plenty of reinforcements, whereas she cannot.

A reckless night for a woman means that she could be left pregnant, or with offspring that has no male to provide and protect for it. One night could lead to a (very short) lifetime without safety and security for her and her offspring. As we mentioned above, a pregnant woman, or a woman with offspring, is less likely to survive in the wilderness.

These facts, among many others, are the reason why women have "intuition," or that ability to perceive things that men miss. Let's look at the evolutionary model again, and how a woman would have survived throughout most of human history. The survival of women and their offspring was based on the fact that her mate was also a good provider/protector. This means she had to weed out the Beta Male and Gamma Male suitors. So, the females that were good at reading micro gestures in the face, or perceiving the signs of a high value man, were the ones that would choose the right male. The ones that could not read the subtle facial expressions of men, which denoted high value or low value, were the ones that mated with the wrong males, and probably died in the wilderness without a proper male protector and provider.

Women have to be more highly sensitive to social cues, because in the wilderness it could be the difference between life and death. This is also why women are the "gate keepers" in social interactions, i.e. it is the burden of the male, even today, to prove his value to the woman. This explains why a man's physical appearance is less important to a woman. Sure, a woman wants a physically strong and healthy man, because these traits indicate a man will produce strong and healthy kids. But, a woman is much more attracted to an intelligent man, whose superior intellect and outgoing personality enable him to more easily and efficiently provide and protect for her and her offspring. An intelligent man is also more likely to become the leader of the tribe.

So when it comes to women, safety and security are paramount. She is always looking out for the male that can provide and protect her and her offspring the best, both physically and mentally. This is based not only on his intellect (which is why humor is so important by the way, as it denotes a sharp intellect), but also on his ability to lead other men. If a man is an Alpha Male, he will have other followers, and he will be a leader of men. The best Alphas are the ones that cannot only provide and protect, but also lead, and connect with the people around them. They are truly the "tribal" leaders. Therefore social status has an impact on the attractiveness of a man to a woman. Have you ever seen an ugly guy with a beautiful woman? It happens all the time, and I bet you anything he is an Alpha Male. Being an Alpha Male has less to do with looks, and much more to do with his personality, which an Alpha shows through his confidence, excellence (skills and abilities), and social standing.

There is something very important which we will revisit later based on what we have said: if you make a woman feel unsafe, or insecure, she will never ever talk to you again. File this into your neocortex for later.

Because looks don't matter as much for women, while women have the social advantage while they are younger and physically attractive, men tend to gain an advantage as they get older. This is why women are often attracted to older men, at least at some point in their lives. Age traditionally correlates with higher social status, as well as confidence, and therefore a higher ability to provide and protect. Men, no matter who they are, always have the burden of proof on them; that is, they always have to prove that they can provide and protect their women, and their offspring.

Even today, this wiring is at work. It is interesting that in modern times, women don't need the provision and protection of men like they used to. Today, women can work, and provide and protect for themselves, which is why so many choose Beta and Gamma males, or choose to raise kids on their own. But, the old wiring is still there, and no woman wants a guy who is a pushover, or an asshole that beats the everlovin' crap out of her or the kids. She is still wired to love high value providers and protectors.

Of course, as we mentioned, the Gamma can, at least for a time, pass as an Alpha, because aggressiveness and assertiveness look a lot alike on the surface. A lot of women, even today, get duped into procreating with a Gamma, only to see their survival put into jeopardy.

Chapter Four: Your Inner Disposition/Inner Game

It is very important for us to understand this brain wiring, to understand why certain strategies work, and why some don't. If you really think about the previous chapter and what it means, then you can understand why women naturally prefer Alpha Males, why they are repulsed by passive Beta Males, and why Gammas, though successful in the short term, are bad news in the long term.

Before we go on to some more practical things, let's highlight the most important point to take away right now: the burden is on the male to prove his worth and value to the female. Women are attracted to high value men, i.e. good providers and protectors. Value comes from intellect, excellence (ability and skills), the ability to connect (empathy), leadership, and more importantly confidence. Physiology, that is, physical appearance is actually pretty low on the scale, when compared to these other things (although it would be unwise to ignore your appearance completely). Of course, a woman will never admit that, because they think that physical appearance is more important than it actually is. Trust us, looks, while more important initially, are not that important overall.

So, what do you need to do to make yourself a high value, attractive male that communicates to a woman that you can provide and protect her and her offspring? The first thing you have to do, which we mentioned in the first chapter, is to believe that you are high value. If you don't believe it, then neither will she. As we mentioned above, one of the ways to convince yourself of your value, is to focus on what you are excellent at. Excellence is one of those "confidence factories," because if you know you are excellent at something, then you will also be confident about it. That means that your inner dialogue, your inner game, and how you deal with yourself is of utmost importance.

The Tao of Steve

We at The Joe Alpha Factor like to deal first in concepts, and then in practicalities. So if your inner game is off, then your ability to talk to anyone, and to be attractive, will also be off. Back in 2000, a movie came out that you should probably see. Go buy it. Play it once a month, forever. It is called <u>The Tao of Steve</u>. <u>The Tao of Steve</u> is a movie about a fat slob named Steve, with a scraggly red beard, who was fantastic with women. If you want to see proof of many of the things that we have discussed so far, then watch that movie. If not, watch it anyway, as it is very true to life with all of our experiences at The Joe Alpha Factor.

In the movie, the "hero," Steve has a threefold approach to getting women to pursue him. While it is not exhaustive of The Joe Alpha Factor philosophy, it certainly is a good way to form your mental inner game. The three factors of the "Tao of Steve" are: *be desireless, be excellent, and be gone.*

1. <u>Be Desireless</u>

Desire gets in the way. Have you ever liked a girl so much that you did dumb crap and you lost her? Or wanted to pass a test so bad, that you freaked out, and failed? Or wanted a job so bad that you messed up the interview? The science that we base our philosophy on has a negative outlook on desire. Dr. Jeffery Schwartz, for instance, in his book <u>You Are Not Your Brain</u>, says that desire gives us unrealistic expectations and disappointments when we either achieve or don't achieve our goals. Dr. David Lieberman, another favorite author of ours, says that desire and confidence are *inversely* proportional. That means the more desire you have, the less confident you will be about getting what you desire, and the less likely you will get that object of your desire.

While "desire" is a perfectly good word, we at The Joe Alpha Factor prefer to use the word "attachment." "Desire" isn't all bad. I can desire to be a more confident and outgoing person. If we generalize and say that all desire is bad, then even the desire to eat could be construed as bad. Rather, we reframe "desire" as attachment. The more I am attached to something, the more emotion I will have over the possibility of either losing it, if I have it, or not getting it, if it is the object of my attachment.

This is where the "Law of Scarcity," comes in. In his book <u>Influence</u>, Robert Cialdini talks about the human tendency of getting nervous or anxious when something is scarce. This comes, of course, from evolution, as scarcity in the wild often meant death, and the more scarce something is, the more attached we get to it. So, when we are attached it usually means we are afraid we are going to lose something, and so we react with anxiety, and lack of confidence.

What is more, David Lieberman says when we get attached to something, we get hyper-focused on it, and we begin to believe that our survival (there is that word again) becomes dependent on having that thing in our life. We begin to hyper-focus on that object to the detriment of everything around us, which in turn creates anxiety and lack of confidence, two things that hinder the chances of achieving what we wanted in the first place!

Thus, while it seems counter-intuitive, being hyper-attached to something means we are *more* likely to lose the object of our attachment. This is why detachment is so important. By detachment, we mean "emotional" detachment. This is one of those times when emotional attachment can be our downfall. When our emotions get involved, which are there to help us to not only connect, but survive, we begin to get very nervous about losing the thing we are attached to.

How do you know if you are attached? Think about living without that thing. If you get anxious or nervous, and perhaps nauseous, you are attached. If you can't easily walk away from something, you are attached. Detachment, then, means that you have to force yourself to walk away. It is odd, but the women whom I have been detached from have all followed after me. Heck, they have *chased* after me. The Law of Scarcity works both ways.

Detachment gives you the flexibility to keep your wits about you. If you are emotionally attached to a girl, you will probably freak her out, make a mistake, or lose your confidence (which is the worst thing), which in turn will lower your value in her eyes. Walking away from this situation will end up restoring your confidence in the end. You can't be "excellent" if you are anxious and nervous. Think of the quintessential confident hunks in the movies. They don't care at all if a woman likes them or not. They are completely detached, which is why women end up chasing after them.

How do you get detached? Simply acknowledging that you are attached has a lot of value in moving you toward detachment. Acknowledging the emotion of attachment (and really ANY negative emotion) tends to cut it in half. If you acknowledge attachment, then ask yourself *why* you are attached. Do not approach *any* woman in an attached state. You will just be wasting your time. A lot of time attachment comes from what we call "approach anxiety," which comes from your brain telling you that you will die if you approach the wrong girl. If you approach full of approach anxiety, you will just blow it, and fail to meet your dream girl.

Detachment is difficult to attain, but achieving it, even partially, will bring you a lot of success. Just remember, everyone is practice. You will not die from an approach, and you will not die if you don't get a particular girl. Remember, there are three billion other ones out there.

Moby Dick

I think a literary reference may be helpful to show how deadly attachment can be. Herman Melville wrote a book in 1851 that we are probably all familiar with, at least in concept, called <u>Moby Dick.</u> I have never actually read the book, as it is super long, but I have seen movies or references about it all of my life. I think we can all know what the novel is about: a man who is completely obsessed with killing the white whale, Moby Dick.

Captain Ahab, one of the main characters, had a run-in with the white whale in his past, which left him scarred and bitter. He dedicated the rest of his whaling career to hunting down, and killing, the white whale out of revenge.

Throughout the story, we see how this attachment to revenge consumes Captain Ahab, and eventually leads to the destruction of his ship, the death of his crew, and even his own demise. The important part of the book is that attachment affects judgment in a negative way.

The same is true if we find ourselves attached to a girl, or an idea. The more fixated I am on a particular girl (my "white whale"), the less likely I am to be in an intimate relationship with me. The attachment will cloud my judgment, make me second and third guess my decisions, and reduce my ability to be excellent.

Again, this is not true for a particular girl, but is true with just about anything in life. What if I am attached to the "idea" that I have to have a girlfriend in my life, or else I will die? Women can smell desperation from a mile away, and it repulses them. The same is true if you are desperate for a job, for instance. Who will be calmer in an interview, the man who has $100,000 in savings and is interviewing for the job, or the guy who is on unemployment? Of course, one will be calmer, more excellent, and more detached, and will probably get the job.

I think an example would be good here. When I was in Junior High, I was awkward around girls, just like every other Junior High kid. I had a crush on this girl named Laura since the 6th grade. She was cute, funny, and I liked her very much. I always felt so weird around her, because I didn't want to screw things up or say the wrong thing. One day I got the courage to call her on the phone and ask her out. This was the 8th grade. It took me *two* years to finally call her. She picked up the phone and I asked her out in the most awkward way possible. I should have won the award for awkwardness. She said "no," and I simply said: "That works," and hung up the phone. It was an awkward next day in biology class we took. Plus, I sat behind her (because I did creepy stuff like that) and had to endure the embarrassment of that weird phone call.

At the same time, there was a girl I sat next to in band, whose name was Mary. Mary and I were friends. She was cute enough, but all my focus and attention was on Laura. Mary and I would joke around, make fun of the other guy in the section, and the band director. Mary was fun to hang out with, and there was no pressure. My mom always dropped me off a couple of hours early to school, and I had to sit in the cafeteria finding ways to entertain myself until my friends arrived at school. Mary would usually show up and we would hang out. It was really great. I think about Mary a lot to this day.

When it came time to sign my yearbook, which was the summer before I moved to another city, Laura wrote a little bit, and Mary wrote a lot. When I look back at that yearbook, I realize how much Mary liked me. My attachment to Laura made me miss out on what probably could have been my first girlfriend.

As a follow-up, years later on Facebook I looked for both. I never found Mary (she would never have been the type to get on Facebook anyway) and I thought that I couldn't find Laura either. I shrugged my shoulders and moved on with life. It was a few months after that, that I realized Laura and I were already friends on Facebook! She had a different name due to marriage, so I never recognized her when she friended me (I accept all requests). In the end, years later, Laura searched *me* out! Life is a crazy thing.

The reason that Mary liked me was because of my detachment toward her. I acted normally around her, had rapport with her, and didn't worry about what I was supposed to say. I try to act that way around anyone I meet to this day. I thank Mary for teaching me the lesson of detachment.

If you find yourself attached and fixated on someone, or something, or even an idea of something you need to have, walk away, look at things from a bigger perspective and context, and realize that life without her, or that thing, will not mean your death. In other words, if you want something, you have to not really care if you get. Yeah, it sounds contradictory, but that is how it works!

Detachment helps you to have control of your mental faculties, because as long as you are being controlled by emotion, desire, and attachment, you will not have the tranquility of mind to be focused. When you remain detached, that means that you can move on to the second step of the "Tao of Steve," Be Excellent.

2. Be Excellent

People are attracted to excellence. Excellence, as defined in <u>The Simpsons</u>, is the "act or state of being excellent." Of course, that doesn't really tell us much does it?

The important thing here is that excellence is attractive. Excellence can really be thought of as an ability to perform an act or skill, mixed with confidence. When we are excellent, we are using our gifts and talents at our highest ability, and we know that we are using them in the best way possible, which in turn means that we are using them confidently.

Think about something you are good at. We are all good at something, right? We all have something we like to do, even if it is play video games, that we know that when we are engaging in that activity, we are being the best we can be. For me, it is public speaking (well, there are a lot of things I am excellent at, but that is *the* best one). When I am speaking in front of a crowd, I know what I am doing. I know how to get their attention, how to inflect my voice, and what to say, mostly without thinking. It is something I can just flip on.

Perhaps you are different. I guarantee you are. Maybe you are good with kids, or maybe you are an artist. Maybe you can fix computers, bench press 400 pounds, or run a half-marathon. Maybe it is even magic. Whatever you are good at, if you can demonstrate that you are excellent with confidence, you will be attractive.

Alpha Males are confident in whatever they do. They are always excellent, not to impress people, or win people over (since they are naturally detached from that), but they are excellent for excellence sake. They are excellent when people are not looking, and that excellence in a primary skill bleeds over into other areas of their life.

I imagine that Arnold Schwarzenegger is not good at everything. No one can be, but you would never know that, since his confidence comes from the fact he knows what he is good at. It certainly carries over into other areas of his life. Excellence and confidence are always related to each other. He knows what he is good at, confidently does that thing, and gives himself the boost of confidence he needs to be the Super Alpha that he says he is.

Excellence works the same way for all of us. If we find what we are really good at, and do that thing to a level of excellence, that confidence will spill over into every area of our lives.

What is important for our purposes is that excellence is attractive. Why is that? It is a demonstration of value. People are attracted to high value people. Michael Jordan was excellent at basketball, and that confidence spilled over into everything he did, making him loved by millions of people. Incidentally, when he was attached to the idea of playing baseball, and was not good at it, he walked away (became detached) and went back to basketball, where he was excellent again.

Not all women or men find the same things attractive. People all have their tastes in life, but all people are attracted by confidence and excellence. Here is an example: There is a YouTube video of a girl stacking cups. She is the fastest cup stacker in the whole world. She is followed by millions of people, and probably makes a lot of money stacking cups. There is no doubt that when it comes to cup-stacking, she is confident, detached, and excellent, and because of that she has attracted millions of people to watch her stack cups. It no doubt has attracted wealth and fame as well. And all she does is stack cups! This just shows you that excellence can be found in anything, and second, that even the most mundane talent can make you attractive.

That being said, we should not be excellent in a way that repulses people. Don't be that chess nerd that only talks about chess, or the sports fan that always drones on about baseball stats. That is the sign of attachment. Rather be the guy who is excellent at chess or baseball, and can carry that excellence into other things that he does, who can generalize excellence into his daily life, even if it isn't his chief skill in life.

Women are always attracted to excellence. Of course, going back to our evolutionary model from before, an excellent male was capable of providing and protecting, and offering safety and security in the jungle. Excellence in an area demonstrates all the things that attract women to men: intellectual ability, confidence, attraction, and value.

Returning to the idea of the Tao of Steve, being excellent in her presence is a vital part of attracting her to you, and for you to demonstrate confidence and ability. This plays out in every area of your life. People love value, and being excellent demonstrates that you are both valuable and attractive. This is why teenage boys "show off" to teenage girls - they are trying to demonstrate excellence, so that they can later "mate" with them. Notice I said *trying* because most end up failing because they try too hard (attachment).

It is important to note that not all ways of being excellent fit with every environment. We will be talking more about environments in Part IV of this book. For instance, I would not whip out a chess board if you are in a dance club, nor would I try to shoot hoops in a coffee shop. Sometimes you need to be excellent, capture that feeling of excellence, and take it with you into other environments. You can even discuss, in an indirect way, your excellence if you can't demonstrate it directly. We will cover that later.

The nice thing about all environments is that there are always Alphas in every environment and field, and that means that there will be women attracted to them. Michael Jordan is the Alpha in his field. Gary Kasperov is the Alpha in the field of Chess. Einstein was the Alpha in the field of science. They all attracted women to them.

You may need to stay within your environment to meet the right women. For instance, don't go to a dance club and talk about your extensive knowledge of Star Trek to the most beautiful girl in the room, because she probably won't know Captain Kirk from Captain Morgan. But do that to the cute girl at the Star Trek convention and it may work in your favor. Being excellent, however, is more about a state of mind, which you need to carry with you at all times, and that flows from your ability to be excellent. There are some demonstrations of excellence that will work, however, for both the girl in the club *and* the girl at the Star Trek Convention. We will cover those in Part IV, so be sure to keep reading.

So here is an idea. Before you go out to meet women, or before you go out to do anything, do something that you are excellent at. Notice the feeling of confidence that comes with it, and carry that feeling into every interaction throughout your day, no matter whom you are interacting with.

3. <u>Be Gone</u>

In the movie, Steve rightly quotes Martin Heidegger when he says: "we pursue that which flees from us."

He is absolutely right for a variety of reasons. First, let's look at the other two numbers here in the Tao. Being gone includes the other two. It is a demonstration of detachment: if you cannot walk away from something, then you are probably not detached. That means you are probably hyper-focusing on the thing you want, which erodes confidence and your ability to be excellent. If you find yourself in this position, walking away may be the toughest thing that you have to do, but in the bigger picture, it may be exactly what you need to do to return to a state of excellence.

I know there are times when I have really liked a girl, so much that it hurt. I was attached to her deeply, and I wanted to call her and text her. It made my brain hurt, I was so attached. How do you think I sounded when I talked to her? I probably sounded needy and desperate (yep, it happens even to the best of us).

So, what did I do? I walked away. I told myself I would not talk to her, text her, or even answer her texts or calls! It hurt like hell! Again, my brain was on fire, and it actually hurt in my body! But after a short time, it started to hurt less, I was able to focus on being excellent in other areas of my life, and I returned to a state of confidence.

And then, she called me, and started texting me, to the point that *she* looked needy and desperate. I have to say, that happens a lot when I am detached, excellent, and gone. They usually chase me!

Let me note something very important: this "Tao" is useful in two ways. First, if you really want to attract a girl, then you have to be these three things, and second, if you want to *get over* a girl that has hurt you, especially your "Moby Dick," you have to be them as well. I have counseled men and women in break-ups with this philosophy, and, if they follow this philosophy, what ends up happening is that they start to get chased by their ex! In the end, they become detached enough to have the flexibility and freedom to let that person back in their lives, or not. Sometimes we just need to walk away from someone or something to get a little perspective.

Why does "being gone" thing work? Well, I think the answer can be found in the book, <u>Influence</u>, by Robert Cialdini, which I have referenced already. Get that book. Read it. Love it. It was a game changer for me.

Remember the "law of scarcity" mentioned earlier? Cialdini cites a study in which people were asked to rate the taste of cookies, but with a twist. Some subjects were given the impression that they were eating the last available cookies, while others believed there were lots of cookies left. Even though they were the same cookies, people rated them as tastier when there were fewer cookies in front of them, as opposed to when the cookies were plentiful. "Scarcity" actually made the cookies taste better, and the subjects perceived their value as higher!

This probably comes from evolutionary programming, because when we were out in the forest or the jungle, all resources were scarce, so we had to really focus and pursue anything that came our way. Since basic, life-giving resources were often scarce, we have come to highly value scarce things, and to be conscious of them, how to obtain them, and how to use them.

It follows then that when things are scarce, they engage this evolutionary part of our minds, and the survival part of our brains kicks in, and alerts us to the scarce resources. Remember, our brains are wired the way they are because of survival, so the brain that could recognize resources as scarce, and then act to obtain those scarce resources, passed down their genetic material and wiring.

So, when you "are gone," it kicks in that same set of evolutionary constructs in the other person's brain. That part that says, "Uh-oh, I had better do what I can to keep this scarce resource around." In the body language section of this book, we talk about "false time constraints," and body language that indicates you may be leaving at any moment. We'll show you ways to make women worry about the "threat" that you, a scarce and excellent resource, may be going away.

Remember, in the study mentioned above, when a cookie was seen as "scarce," people rated the cookie as more pleasant, tastier, and more valuable than the cookies that were perceived as abundant. "Being gone," does the same thing, especially if you have already demonstrated excellence. It makes an already valuable resource scarce, which helps to make you seem even *more* valuable. And as we said above, it also makes you more able to be detached from a situation, which ensures clear thinking and good decision making, and lets you continue to be excellent for excellence sake.

Inner Game

None of the other stuff we are going to present in this book is going to work if you don't have the appropriate state of mind. You can have a confident body posture, but if you are wracked with worry from attachment, it will come across just as it is: fake.

So before you do anything, you need to put yourself in a proper state of mind, a state of detached excellence that allows you to be the best you can be, for the sake of being the best you can be. You cannot *force* people to be attracted to you, but if you are excellent, you will naturally attract people, wealth, jobs, and anything else you may need to have a happy and excellent life.

We will present other "mental game" techniques in this book, especially in the body language section, and the section about overcoming approach anxiety.

Central to being an Alpha Male is being attractive to EVERYONE. Yes, everyone, not just women.

You have to be the man that men want to be and follow, and the man every woman sees as valuable enough to spend their time with. You must be the man that provides and protects, and that attracts people and resources. To be a successful Alpha Male, and be successful in any area of life, it is absolutely necessary to have a confident frame of mind. There are many concepts related to a solid inner "game" that we have presented here, and there are many others, but this is a good start. So go, be excellent, feel excellent, and let that feeling permeate everything you do in life.

Part II: Overcoming Approach Anxiety

Chapter Five: Approach Anxiety

I suspect every dude has been there at least once (well, maybe a thousand times) in his life. He is at the coffee shop or the grocery store, maybe in a club or a bar with friends, or at school or work, and he sees that perfect woman. The one who is just his type, with the perfect face, nice laugh, good personality, or the one that just looks super-good looking and gets his motor running. In his mind he thinks about taking her out on a date, getting to know her, or maybe even more! Then the fear wells up. It happens to the best of us, that fear we like to call *approach anxiety*. Approach anxiety in his brain shoot off all sorts of warning endorphins, giving him all the reasons why approaching a woman of this caliber might just end his life.

He thinks about how she might shoot him down, how he might feel if she says "no," and what the other people at work or in the coffee shop might think. Then the excuses come. "Well, I can't talk to her now because I am on the way to the meeting." "A girl like that would never ever talk to me." "I bet she has a boyfriend." "Those people standing near her are in my way." I even knew a guy who refused to approach a beautiful girl because she was his "grandma's neighbor as a child," and apparently interacting with her would somehow be inappropriate because of that! As you can see, these excuses are about as pathetic as they get, but the brain still plays these awful tricks that seem very real. So, even though he wants to, he goes on without ever talking to the girl. Even if he sees her every day at the same class or meeting, he just sits there, hoping *she* will break the ice and come to *him*.

We have all been there. Every guy has experienced approach anxiety at some point in his life, even if he is the most confident weight lifter, handsome movie star, or Green Beret. Approach anxiety affects us all, and for some, it is permanently paralyzing. And you know what the kicker is? It is perfectly natural! That's right; approach anxiety is built into our brain wiring! What the hell?!

It all goes back to the wild, to our primate ancestors who roamed the jungle looking for food, fleeing from predators, and most importantly, trying to have babies with each other. Making kids is part of the very genetic makeup of who we are, which means sex is at the very core of our identity. This is why men think about sex all the time (you knew there had to be a good reason!): they are trying to make themselves "immortal" through their offspring. Sex is on women's minds too, but in a very different way that we will cover later.

So what is the deal with this approach anxiety then? If we want to have sex, and we want to have kids, what is the big deal? Why would our brains be wired to make us afraid to approach a member of the opposite sex? The answer, hinted at in the previous paragraph, is survival.

Survival goes both ways. Not only do we want to be "immortal" through the creation of offspring, we also have to survive long enough to do that! That means we have an aversion to being killed. I personally know that I hate being killed, so I avoid being killed at all costs. Being killed is one of my least favorite things, but women, are some of my favorite things!

In our tribal days, when humans and other primates were running around in tribes of 50-150 (at the most), getting a date was even harder than today. Do the math: if there is a tribe of 50 people, only about eight of the 25 females are at the age to reproduce. The others are too old or too young. That means that you are competing with ten to fifteen other men for eight females! What if they are taken? What if you approach the female of the big chief who can clobber you to death? If you do, he *will* clobber you to death! So you have a reason to be cautious about whom you approach.

So, approach anxiety is built into our brains as a way to survive, so we might find the right woman with whom to procreate and have kids. The problem is that for a number of guys, approach anxiety is very difficult to overcome, and even, as we mentioned, paralyzing. The men that overcome approach anxiety get to procreate, and the ones that don't live a lonely existence. So that little fear, and all those excuses that come into your mind when you see the girl of your "dreams," is perfectly normal and natural. But, if you don't want to sleep alone for the rest of your life, you have to overcome it. And the good news is that it IS possible to overcome.

Before we go on to how this works, let's talk about women for a second. They have approach anxiety too, but it is different from us men. Women get approach anxiety when they are approached! Have you ever walked up to a girl in a bar, or in a coffee shop, and when you said something to her, she just gave you that cold stare until you left? Well, that is her approach anxiety kicking in. Think about moving too quickly around a cat (women are a lot like cats); it will freeze up until the threat is gone, and if it feels threatened enough, will even run away! And finally, it will turn and fight, if necessary.

Women need to survive too. Evolution has built survival into their brains as well. But remember, women are typically shorter, smaller, and weaker than men. This means that back when we were in the wild, women had a greater chance of being eaten by a wild animal, or even stolen by a competing tribe, than did men. So women have to be extra cautious themselves. If you approach her, because of our brain wiring, she is more likely to perceive you as a threat, meaning that she will first see you as a foe, rather than a friend. She has to do this, because in the wild, if she were approached by a foe, she could have gotten hurt, killed, or worse. So, your initial job, when it comes to women, is to overcome their approach anxiety, which means you have to overcome your own.

Imagine how a girl might react if an anxious guy, sweating, nervous, and stiff, approaches her in any situation. Her defense mechanisms, i.e. her "approach anxiety," will kick in, and she will wonder what is wrong with this guy. She might shut down and stare, or if she feels threatened, she may actually verbally attack this poor schlub. Let me say it again: if you want to overcome her natural anxiety, you have to overcome yours.

The good news is that you can overcome approach anxiety. It is clearly possible; otherwise there would be no people in the world, because men would never approach women! And that is the difference between you and the guy that gets the girl: he overcame his approach anxiety.

It is important to note that you can never fully "get over" approach anxiety. The most potent Alpha Male in the group, the leader of the pack, still gets approach anxiety. There is still a little part of his brain that is looking out for his survival, and makes him think twice about approaching an attractive girl. The difference between him, and the Beta Male, the passive guy who hopes the girls approach him (which doesn't happen that often), is that the Alpha has learned to use the energy from approach anxiety in his favor, rather than as a handicap. See, when you get approach anxiety, adrenaline starts pumping, and all those flight/fight signals start going off in your head. You can actually turn that energy toward your advantage, and actually come off as more confident and approachable!

In the next few chapters we are going to show you how to directly encounter approach anxiety, to demonstrate that no one, at least in modern times, has ever been killed by rejection. Finally, we will give you some tips on how to overcome, and even utilize to your advantage, the specter known as approach anxiety.

Chapter Six: Death by Rejection?

So before we go on, we should deal with the obstacle known as rejection. Rejection is a part of life. Everyone gets rejected sometime by someone. It sucks. It actually hurts. In fact, scientific research has shown that emotional pain activates the same brain areas as physical pain! But, rejection by a female has never ever killed anyone, ever, at least not directly.

As we covered in the last chapter, we have a desire to survive. Certainly, back in our days running around caves, jungles, and forests, rejection by a woman might have meant that her mate would club you on the head with a rock. Sure, that kind of rejection could kill you. Certainly, there is a slim chance that you could approach the wrong girl in a club who has a drunk jerk of a boyfriend with a gigantic pet rock, but the chance of that in modern times is slim. Besides, the kind of rejection we are talking about here is of an emotional and social nature. I have never seen one guy keel over and die just because he got shot down by a girl. But of course, your brain tells you otherwise.

The Joe Alpha Factor teaches a very simple and important truth about being rejected: *rejection is not death*. In fact, rejection can be a good thing, if you see it in the right way! "What?!" you say. Yes, I would say that rejection has made me the man I am today, who is able to talk to any girl, and really anyone, in any setting.

Look at millionaires and successful business people. Most of them failed in their initial business ventures, and are alive and well to tell about it. Rejection can provide you with a learning experience that helps you in your next approach.

It is important to reframe rejection as not an event that can destroy you, but as a process that can be fun! Having fun with rejection can actually turn the energy generated by approach anxiety into something that is helpful. Some of my favorite stories are about the colossal rejections in our clients' approaches. Most of the time, if they get shot down they just stare at the guy as their own defenses come up. But my favorite stories come from the awesome rejections our clients have received. I love it when they get upset at them now. Usually after they have been trained, they approach in a very confident, and even cocky way, and some women don't react well to that (although most do), and sometimes they say and do things that are hilarious in order to shoot them down.

After all is said and done, when they return after a great shoot down, we usually have a laugh, and try it again. Sometimes, we take guys out to see how many times they can get shot down! Rejection can be reframed into something positive in so many ways. In fact, we rarely talk about the many successes we have, but we have a blast talking about the few, but entertaining, rejections they have experienced. Really, making rejection "fun" shows that you are flexible and confident, and this sort of attitude will actually make you more, not less, attractive to women. Women love flexible and confident men.

So what do you do if you get rejected? Well, deal with it. Be honest with yourself: at the beginning of learning how to approach women, rejection can hurt very badly. It may initially erode your confidence, so the most important thing is to acknowledge that it hurts. Acknowledging your feelings (and yes we have them gents) is the only sure-fire way to guarantee that your feelings don't consume you. If you let your hurt feelings go wild, they will take over, and you will be sitting, and sleeping, by yourself for the rest of your life. The other important thing to realize after a rejection is that you are not dead. It didn't kill you. Rejection will never kill you. If you doubt it, take a deep breath.

The other thing about rejection is that you may strongly fear what other people will think of you if you get rejected in front of a bunch of people. Guess what? No one ever died from embarrassment! If you make a total fool of yourself in a room full of strangers, then remember, they are just that, a room full of strangers. In a club, it is no big deal, since you can leave that club and go to another one where no one knows you, to start fresh. Certainly, the fear of rejection, and the social stigma of rejection increases when there are fewer people in the room, making your rejection more noticeable. Keep in mind that those watching you are only strangers, and if you totally mess up a room, and everyone sees you rejected, laugh it off for what it is, and leave. No one will ever see you again. And if they do, they will remember that you had the guts to at least try to approach, something that most of them probably were too scared to do. Don't forget, when you are spending time overcoming approach anxiety, you want to experience colossal rejections that later turn into great stories for your buddies. Major rejections also provide future conversation topics with the women you will meet. I guess we can cover that in another guide. So if you are rejected by a woman, or laughed out of the room, guess what? YOU WILL SURVIVE, and live to fight another day, richer for the experience.

Before we move on, think about comedians. The funniest guys out there have all been booed off the stage more than we know. Jokes that didn't land, bad crowds, or whatever happened to them, made them the successes they are. The ones that learned from the setbacks became famous. Do you know what happened to the guys who were afraid of being booed off stage? Me neither. They are probably working at a McDonald's somewhere in Idaho. I have done speaking engagements that didn't go well. Those are, again, the best stories, and the experiences that made me the success I am today.

What also follows is that the more you are rejected, the more robust you will become against rejection. Think about this in terms of weight lifting: in order to build your muscles, you have to break them down, and you have to rough them up a little. You have to lift more than they are really capable of lifting. When you do this, the muscles break down, but they build up even bigger. The same is true when we someone rejects us. It actually builds us up. Like I said above, there are actually nights where we take guys out in order to get shot down. It helps them to be more resilient against rejection in the future, as well as giving me some great stories. Of course, the more they do these types of things, and approach rejection with this type of attitude, the less they get shot down and rejected.

Why is that?! Well, women love confident men; they like Alpha Males. Alpha Males are not afraid of anything. They are detached, and they do whatever the next right move is without fear. They roll with the punches. If you make yourself immune to rejection, by exposing yourself to it, the more confident, and therefore attractive, you will become. It is the same concept as a vaccine: exposure to the virus in a way that won't kill you makes you develop immunity to the actual virus! The Joe Alpha Factor has developed techniques, which will be shared in the upcoming chapter, on how to achieve this immunity against rejection, and actually enjoy getting shot down! The more immunity from rejection you develop, the more successful you will be with women. I bet you are actually excited to get rejected by now! I know I am.

The most important concept you can take from the experience of rejection is another important truth we teach at The Joe Alpha Factor: *there is no failure, just feedback*. This is an important principle to memorize and utilize in every aspect of your life, not just with women. If you remove "failure" from your active vocabulary, there is nothing to fear. Every experience, easy or hard, fun or not, painful or painless, has something to teach you.

Remember when I mentioned that millionaires, comedians, and business people have all failed at least once in their life? So has every man that has ever talked to a woman. The men that have truly mastered the art of approaching women have probably failed more times than you know or can imagine. Rejection is not "bad," but rather an experience that can teach what not to do next time you approach. The more rejection you encounter initially means far less rejection later. That is because with every rejection, you learn something: you get feedback on how to stand, how to talk, how to read their signs of attraction or signs that they are not attracted. With every rejection, you will actually find more success. So embrace it. It won't ever kill you, just make you stronger, faster, and better. It will also give you more material to roll out when talking to people. Besides, everyone loves a good shoot down story, especially when the guy who got shot down doesn't seem to be affected negatively by it!

Chapter Seven: Techniques to Reduce Approach Anxiety

Now comes the practical stuff: how do we overcome approach anxiety, and turn it from something that paralyzes us, to something that will actually HELP us meet women? As we covered in the last chapter, the first thing we need to do is to reframe, that is to see rejection as a whole in a different and positive way. We discussed in the last chapter that we at The Joe Alpha Factor actually embrace rejection as a way to make ourselves more robust, to teach us what works and what doesn't, and to give us some great stories about rejection that later turn our anxiety about approaching women into a strength, and ultimate success. So what if she shoots you down? That means you will be better for the next girl that comes along, and more confident to approach her.

There are some other techniques that we have discovered or developed to help the Ben Betas of the world turn into Joe Alphas. Some of the techniques that follow should be practiced by yourself before you leave the house, and others should be practiced in field.

The Testosterone "Instaboost"

Testosterone is one hell of a drug! It is what makes men, men. High testosterone men are assertive, competitive, confident, and attractive to women. All men have testosterone surging through our bodies, at varying levels, and the more we have, the easier it will be to overcome approach anxiety in the long run. Even successful women, such as those high-powered women that are managing businesses, have higher levels of testosterone than other women. So how does a man "boost" his testosterone? Well, there are, of course, artificial ways to do it, such as steroids, but that comes with a cost, namely insanity, 'roid rage, cancer, and general douchbagness.

Over the course of our research into human behavior, we have come upon research, from Harvard and Columbia, that concludes there is a way to boost your testosterone levels naturally, thus giving you the edge to convert approach anxiety into confidence. We call it the "testosterone instaboost," and it is something we have practiced with great results.

We know that the mind affects the body. If you are feeling depressed mentally, you will release physical chemicals that correspond to that feeling of depression. If you are in love, you will release dopamine, endorphins, and all sorts of chemicals in your brain as well. But this mind-body relationship is not a one way street, so what we do with our bodies also affects our mental states. That is where the "instaboost" comes in. Studies have proven that if we want to change our mental mood, sometimes all we have to do is to change our physical posture.

For instance, it is impossible for us to smile, and not feel better. Why is that? Well, even when we aren't in a great mood, and we choose to smile, the brain has to do all sorts of operations for that smile to occur. Normally, we smile naturally when we are in a good mood. So when we smile (even when we are not in a good mood) the brain has connected smiling with a good mood. So in order for the brain to do all the normal operations to smile, it also starts to think it is in a good mood, so you start to feel better. Thus if you are in a crappy mood, smiling will force your brain to release all the chemicals that are associated with feeling good. So the mind affects the body, but the body also affects the mind.

So what does this have to do with testosterone and all sorts of other chemicals that have to do with confidence and assertiveness?

The same thing applies to other body postures as we discussed with smiling, above. If you want to feel more confident, take a confident pose. When you take the "Rocky Balboa" pose (arms raised in the air as if you just conquered the world), your brain has to do all sorts of operations to make that confident pose happen, so it naturally says to itself, if I am doing this confident pose, I must be in a confident mood, and releases the appropriate chemicals, including testosterone, adrenaline, endorphins, and other positive chemicals. The more you "pose" like this, the more chemicals get released, and the more chemicals released, the more confident you will feel. If you *act* bulletproof, you will *feel* bulletproof.

This should be practiced every day. Holding a powerful pose for a minute or two a day will tell your brain you are a confident person, and you will act accordingly. One very powerful pose, which is easy to do anywhere, is to sit at a desk or table and spread your arms out very wide, to claim as much space as possible. This little act increases testosterone. Holding confident poses should especially be practiced before you go out to meet women, for job interviews, or whatever situation demands confidence.

Have you ever seen a guy walk into a room with slumped shoulders? That is not the guy I want playing on my rugby team. That is the secondary effect of this: the more confident posture you express, the more other people will perceive you as confident, and confidence is attractive. The more attractive you feel the more attractive you will be! Being attractive is a choice!

In The Field: Open Focus And The Shoot Down Set

The Open Focus Technique

OK so now you are mentally and physically ready to go out, but you will still encounter approach anxiety. Everyone does, even the most confident Alpha Males. So there are two techniques in the field that you can use.

The first is called "Open Focus." Dr. David Lieberman, in his book, Get Anyone To Do Anything, tells us that the more hyper-focused on something someone is, the less confident they will be that they will get it. In other words, confidence and desire are inversely proportional. When you start to hyper focus, in a negative way, on a girl, the likelihood that you will actually talk to her or get her, will go downhill. So the "open focus" technique is a way to widen your focus, become more detached, have less desire, and more confidence generally.

The Open Focus technique was developed by Dr. Les Fehmi, and explained in the excellent book The Open Focus Brain. It is used by NFL football players, musicians, and other performers. It is a way of seeing the big picture and not letting one or two details get you down. The idea, basically, is to focus on, or imagine, "nothing." For instance, an easy way to do this is to imagine the space between words on this very paragraph. Did it even occur to you that the spaces were even there, even though there are thousands of them in this book alone? Try it. Take a second to focus on the empty space between the words or even the letters, and you will notice your muscles relaxing, and your breathing slow down. Your vision will also widen, as you notice a larger "field of view." You will notice colors get brighter and things come more into focus.

The mind cannot conceptualize "nothing," and so it "takes a break" and shuts down for a second, causing your body to relax. You can focus on the space in an empty beer bottle, or even the space between your eyes, not your eyes or your nose themselves, but the "space" between them. Again, this makes the mind focus on "nothing," since empty space is not something you can conceptualize.

If you are feeling a lot of anxiety while "in the field," simply try this technique, which can be done any time, and anywhere, to help you relax. Take a second and imagine empty space, "nothing." Sometimes I do it when I am stopped at a stoplight, and use the space between the two stoplights, or the space between tail lights of the car in front of me.

The Shoot Down Set

Another great technique that is exclusive to The Joe Alpha Factor is called the "Shoot Down Set." When we go out into the field, even for those of us experienced with social interaction, we still get a little approach anxiety. The "Shoot Down Set" is a sure fire way to eject approach anxiety for the night, and to get some adrenaline shooting through your system.

Here it is: at the very beginning of the evening, as soon as you see a group of girls, go up to them and say: "Shoot Me Down." Go expecting to be shot down. Go into the interaction wanting to be shot down. If they shoot you down, then they did exactly what you wanted. Success! Most won't shoot you down though. It is funny, because some of the best interactions our clients get all evening are during the Shoot Down Set.

Generally, you will get a weird look, because no one ever says that to them. Most girls are nice, and the only reason they shoot people down is that they are simply worrying about their safety, as we discussed above. The Shoot Down Set blows past their defenses.

Some will shoot you down; most will laugh, or ask you what the heck you mean. When they ask you what it means, you have a chance to explain what you are doing, and strike up a conversation. Since they asked you to explain yourself further, their defenses have gone down. Congrats: you just conquered your approach anxiety and theirs at the same time! See why this technique is absolute gold?

This works... it works too well, sometimes! The reason is that you are walking into the situation expecting to get shot down, so you go in detached, and confident. You don't care if they shoot you down, because that it what you asked them to do! And if they don't shoot you down, that means that you are talking to girls now! Either way, your approach anxiety will be nullified, because your brain will begin to realize that you are not going to be killed from the interaction or from rejection. It will make you impervious to being shot down. In fact, in most cases, it will make you want to approach more groups of women, because your testosterone, adrenaline, endorphins, and dopamine will be kicking off in your head! Shoot Down Sets are always fun!

When we are formally training Ben Betas to be Joe Alphas, this is a vital part of our training. We actually have a night out in the field where we go to clubs and bars called the "shoot down night." The task of our clients is to get shot down by at least twenty women. It is daunting at first, as the men have to face their approach anxiety head on. This is what tends to happen: They get shot down. Maybe twice. By the third or fourth group of girls, the approach anxiety is gone, and they end up approaching confidently, and detached for the rest of the night. Many of our clients find it difficult to actually get shot down by twenty groups of women. In fact, it almost never happens. Most of the women end up having a good time too! Plus, if the guys do get shot down, the adrenaline and all those other chemicals are already firing, and it makes them ready for the next set of girls.

Some More "Traditional" Methods of Overcoming Approach Anxiety

The Three Second Rule

The three second rule is a good one, and should be adopted by everyone. The premise of the three second rule is that you have three seconds from visual contact to make the approach. That is so you don't over-think the approach or the interaction, or look too creepy by standing around. Once your pesky brain gets involved, it starts to think of all the ways that it could get rejected, and also ways to preserve itself from the pain of rejection. The three second rule is basically a reminder not to over-think because over-thinking kills.

Just Say Anything!

This rule corresponds to the three second rule. Sometimes you just need to say something to start the conversation, even if it isn't particularly witty. It may just be an observation about what book the girl is reading, what package you are next to in the store, the color of her shoes, or whatever.

How many times has a man stood there wishing he could just say anything to a girl, and when she walks away, he regrets letting her pass. Sure you might get shot down, or she may give you a weird look, or ignore you... or you could meet your future wife. Of course, nothing will happen if you say nothing at all. Let me repeat that: saying nothing is a guaranteed way to lose the game. Again, this is something you can go out to practice: just go out and start talking to random people, men and women, and your approach anxiety will be lessened in the long run.

We at The Joe Alpha Factor believe that one of the hardest things to do with someone you want to talk to is breaking the ice, so just break it. Even if it doesn't make sense and you get a weird look from her, she may just ask you what the heck you meant! You had better have something to say after that, but we will cover that in another Joe Alpha Factor Guide. Again, to recap, to meet a woman in *any* situation, just say something!

Chapter Eight: Final Thoughts On Approach Anxiety

We hope that you can learn to have fun approaching people, especially women in the future. A little different way of thinking, such as reframing rejection as a good thing, can go a long way toward that. Dr. Jeffery Schwartz, an expert in neurology and author of <u>You Are Not Your Brain</u>, reminds us that sometimes our brain sends us deceptive messages, that is, our brain is only doing its job and trying to help us to survive, and so it does the best it can to interpret the incoming data for self-preservation. Sometimes these brain messages are true and help us survive, such as when we are being chased by a bear, and sometimes, most of the time, it makes the same conclusion about women, that they will kill us if we make the wrong move.

However, we can overcome these unhelpful automatic thoughts. The key to overcoming approach anxiety so that you can approach any woman (or anybody for that matter) any time you want is to realize that you might be getting some misinformation from your brain. In other words, you must realize that your thoughts are not always "you." No matter how much your brain screams that you should not approach someone, remember that you can overcome that signal, and you don't have to listen to it. The good news is that, according to Schwartz, the more you resist unhelpful automatic thoughts, the easier it becomes to resist them in the future.

The point of meeting people is to make yourself a better person. It is also to make them a better person. If you think of the good of the other person, making them feel better with your presence, forming a new relationship, improving their life in some way with your presence, your approach anxiety will be reduced even more. When you get out of your own head, become detached, and operate so that you improve peoples' lives with your own, you won't have irrational fears about your own survival. Be a man of the people, at all times, no matter whom you are approaching.

This brings us to two Joe Alpha Factor principles that are fundamental to being an Alpha Male. The first is *treat everyone the same*. This is what sets the Alpha apart from the Beta Male. No matter whom you encounter, man or woman, pretty or ugly, smart or dumb, if you treat everyone well, you will always have people around you, and you will be attractive to all. You will also not be nervous approaching the beautiful girl, because you will realize that she is just like everyone else. Just because she is pretty doesn't mean she is really any different from anyone else. People want to be respected and built up. If you do that in a way that is confident, in a way that makes everyone in the whole group feel better, and do it without being needy, you will have to fight people off because everyone will want to be a part of your life.

Remember to see people as people. To truly be an Alpha Male, you must treat everyone, whether the CEO of a Fortune 500 company, a supermodel, or a homeless man on the street, the same.

While you will have to change certain aspects of your interaction based on whom you interact with, you will be amazed at what happens to you when you are gracious to all who cross your path. Especially treat people well who treat you badly. Rise above their low energy tactics, and be the Alpha Male.

One of our other core principles is to remember that *everyone (and every interaction) is "practice."* Remember what we said above, if you approach someone to talk to them and you get shot down, it is practice for the next person you meet. Nothing counts in this world unless you want it to, so practice, practice, practice. When the runner gets to the race, or the football player to the stadium, they run and they play as they practiced. If they practiced with heart, they will play with heart. If they practiced detached, they will play detached. Even if they walk away from a losing game, they will be better for the next game. Everyone is practice, and it only counts unless you want it to, so "practice" being an Alpha Male with everyone you meet, and guess what, you *will* be the Alpha Male with everyone you meet. It will be fun to see the results!

Part III: The Body Language of Attraction

Chapter Nine: The Importance of Body Language

Congratulations! You have learned to talk! Nice work! It only took you ten years to get it right, and you are probably still learning a thing or two about talking. Talking is great. The ability to speak is what makes us capable of conquering monkeys, building tall buildings, having families, plotting the demise of enemies, and even sharing our thoughts with others. Language is one of those fundamental shifts in our evolutionary history that seems, according to a lot of research, to have developed somewhat quickly.

Before all this yakkity yak was going on, before homo sapiens appeared on the earth about 300,000 years ago, hominids communicated in two ways: loud grunting (which some people are happy to still use to this day), and body language. If you watch primates other than humans, this body language is still the main source of primitive communication- even dogs use body language to communicate with us, and with each other. Heck, any animal with a backbone does it, and some without a backbone (such as Beta Males). Of course, my friend, you have a backbone right? Great!

Primates like ourselves use body language in a variety of ways. When a monkey cleans the fleas out of the hair of another monkey, that means love. When a monkey flings poo at another monkey (or at you when you give him a dirty look at the zoo) that probably means he doesn't like you. It is a good guess anyway. Back away from the cage at that point, unless poo flinging is something you are into, in which case, you are reading the wrong book!

Even though we have all these fancy words, so many languages, devices like mobile phones and computers to send them, body language remains at the core of how we express ourselves. Perhaps we don't clean fleas out of people's hair anymore (or maybe you do) to show affection, and probably we don't literally throw poo anymore when we dislike them (although sometimes we give them "shit," right?), but body language remains a central part of how we are wired to communicate.

Let me give you a really quick example. Have you ever received an email from someone or sent an email to someone and they totally misunderstood your "tone?" Or even better, I know that in my experience speaking foreign languages, it is much harder to understand someone over the phone than seeing them in person. Or heck, just speak to someone on the phone who speaks English as a second language! It will be harder to understand each other, simply because you can't see them.

When I was a tour guide in Rome, I met this beautiful Russian girl named Larissa on a bus. She was a PhD in psychology at a Russian university in Moscow. She didn't speak much English, and I didn't speak any Russian, but I took her on a private tour of the city (of course, it wasn't a burden since she was easy on the eyes...Actually, she was super-beautiful!). I was able to describe the sites with a combination of speaking and body language. Guess which one she understood more. When she got back to Russia, she emailed me and told me that her day in Rome with me was the best that she had during her whole trip there. She couldn't understand 90% of what I was verbally "saying," but she understood because I emphasized my body language in my descriptions, pointing, modeling with my hands, and using non-verbal communication to get my point across.

Body language plays more of a part in our day-to-day communications than we probably realize. Some studies say that up to and over 65% of our communication with people is non-verbal. 65%! The other parts of our communication come from voice inflection (up to 25%) and finally the content (about 10%). See <u>What Every Body Is Saying</u> by Joe Navarro for more information. By "content" I mean the actual words you are saying. So it really still comes down to grunting and pointing, even though our grunting has become extremely sophisticated when our brains evolved over the years.

In many ways, I would have to say that learning the art of reading body language has been one of the best weapons in my personal arsenal of being an Alpha Male. That not only counts with women, but in everything I do, whether it is a presentation (to gauge the crowd's response to what I am saying), to business deals and transactions, and even dealing with my family. Learning to read body language will give you the advantage in nearly every single situation in your life.

However, we aren't going to talk about every single situation in your life here. We are going to talk about what you came here to learn about: women. In this book we are going to describe how women use body language to attract, to indicate how well you are doing with her, and how to read *you*! In the last chapter, we are going to describe how you can use body language to make yourself more attractive as well, and also bolster your own confidence and change your mood.

Chapter Ten: How Body Language Works

I would make one hell of a zombie. "What!?" you say. Yea, I said it; I would make a great zombie because I like brains so much. Brains are great, and I hear, full of protein. Not that I have ever eaten any brains. I swear. How did we get on this topic again?

Before we move on to some practical things, I think it is important to understand the "why" behind the "what." That is, I think you will understand how to use the more practical sections of this book if you understand a little bit of the theory behind body language. There are a lot of great resources available to you at the end of this book if you want to get deeper into specifics in the form of a list of books that have helped me, along with my own personal experience.

Our brains are interesting things. I mentioned earlier that there are two parts to our brain that seem to work on two operating systems, and it is worth explaining again. Remember how I mentioned that our brain really consists of two parts, an older part, and the neocortex (the newer part)? By understanding the relationship between these "operating systems," you can see how body language can be a powerful tool to learn how to discern true intention.

The older parts of the brain, which we earlier compared to the Windows operating system, are collectively referred to as "the reptilian brain." Remember, these are shared with reptiles and other lower mammals. They control things like heart beats, and breathing, and take care of things like emotion and processing visual and audio information. There is a lot that goes on in the "Windows" part of the brain.

I also mentioned the second "operating system," which I compared to a Mac, called the neocortex, which is right above and behind your eyes. It is really advanced stuff in comparison to the back of the brain. However, to understand body language we need to understand the back of the brain a little more, specifically the parts of the brain that compose the ancient limbic system, which we pretty much share with other animals and reptiles.

The limbic system is where we are going to spend a little time. We aren't going to get into boring stuff like amygdalae and hippocampi, but what we will say is that the limbic system helps us with our reactions to things, to things happening outside of our heads in the world we encounter, and things that happen inside of our heads, like the thoughts we have.

Remember why our brains are wired? You should know this by now! It is survival. We LOVE surviving. Surviving is one of the things that we do best, and this relates to body language directly. What is the best way to survive? Well, simply put, run away from danger, and run toward things that are good, like food. In other words, run away from bears, and toward fruit trees. That is the way that our limbic system works too! It runs away from danger, and goes toward what it wants and likes. Pretty simple, right?

The situation for us isn't quite as simple, because of the interaction between our older and newer brains. In humans, the older "Windows" part of the brain reacts to thoughts from the newer "Mac" part of the brain the same way that it reacts to danger in the outside world. In other words, if you are being chased by a bear, your body will react in a certain way, and if you are afraid of being rejected by a woman in your head, even though it is just a thought, your body will react the same way! The back of the brain doesn't really know the difference between a dangerous thought, and a dangerous reality, and will react the same way to it. Same goes for positive thoughts, and positive realities: there is no difference in the reaction of the body.

So, how does this biology lesson relate to body language? Well, when the brain encounters things it doesn't like, it causes the body to automatically do the things it needs to do to survive. According to Joe Navarro, author of <u>What Every Body is Saying</u>, there are three reactions to negative (which the brain reads as "dangerous to survival") input: freeze, flight, or fight.

The first is to "freeze," to completely stop movement altogether. The best animal in the animal kingdom to do this is the opossum. He evolved to "play dead," since he can't outrun predators. So instead of fighting or running, he freezes. By doing this, he increases the odds that a predator won't see him, and if he is seen, the predator may assume he is dead. Either way, he gets left alone, and survives. People do this all the time. We call it the "deer caught in the headlights" look. It is like that moment of shock when you tell someone something serious and they just stand there with that dumb look on their face. This response is largely automatic, and a result of the ancient limbic system.

I have already mentioned that women are a lot like cats, and this is the case with body language as well. Once I was explaining this to my 21-year old niece as we were walking in a downtown metropolitan park, when we saw a cat. I ran full bore at the cat while screaming. The cat froze, and just stared at me, and I also stopped to see what it would do. And it continued just to stand there, frozen, for ten minutes. Then my niece told me I was weird for having a staring contest with a cat, and we went and got ice cream. It was good.

The second reaction to negative information is commonly known as "flight." That is where we turn and run as fast as we can away from danger. Think "horror movie." The cute young teenagers that are constantly being hunted down and killed in those movies are always running in the opposite direction from the killer/zombies/monsters. Usually, the killer/zombies/monsters are faster though, and we get to see the cute teenager killed/eaten/mangled on the screen. What fun!

Finally, the third reaction to negative input is to turn and fight. Let's go back to that cat my niece and I saw in the park that day. Had I kept running at it, it would have turned and started to run away, but if I had cornered that little bastard, he would have turned, done that arching thing with its back, standing its hair on end (to look bigger), and hissed at me. Then it probably would have tried to claw the holy hell out of me. Luckily, we went for ice cream instead…but if I ever see that damned cat again, I will get him. But I digress.

Remember, our brains react to real danger and imagined danger the same way. The stuff in the limbic system doesn't know the difference. So if someone, say in a club, approaches a girl and she freezes (and ignores him), or turns her head away (flight), or finally turns and yells at him (fight), we see all the same things happening that that cat did in the park.

Likewise, if you have approach anxiety you will also have similar reactions. You might freeze because the thought of getting shot down tells your limbic system that an ill-fated approach may mean death! Luckily, the limbic system can be overridden by the "Mac" part of the brain, the neocortex, that is if we know what we are doing.

Finally, when we encounter positive input, from the world around us, as well as the thoughts in our head, our body language will move us in a different direction, that is toward the thing we like. Imagine the pizza has just arrived at the house, and it smells so good, and the cheese is melted, and you can feel the heat from the box. Are you going to put that pizza on the table and then turn away from it like you are scared? Of course not! You and anyone in the room are going to smell the aroma, and see the box, and move toward devouring the pizza.

In the same way, when anyone experiences attraction, the body language will shift to moving toward the thing we like. Our feet, head, chest, and everything else, will point in the direction that we want to go. It is no different whether it is a pizza, or a beautiful woman. Also, it is no different if the woman is attracted to you! We will get to that later.

These two aspects of survival run from things you don't like (i.e. that are dangerous) and run toward things that you like, is what body language is all about! If you know this, and how to distinguish between these two signals that everyone (including animals) has, it will give you a serious advantage in all of your dealings. You simply won't waste time on the people that are not attracted to you, and you will be able to figure out which ones *are* attracted to you in everything you do, from job interviews and speeches, to women in coffee shops and clubs. Also, you will be able to project a certain disposition which *makes* you attractive to members of the opposite sex, and for that matter, anyone.

Chapter Eleven: Reading the Room

Now that you have some basic idea of how and why body language operates, it is time to put that information to good use.

Anytime I enter the room, I size it up. I try to figure out who is together, how long they have been together, whether they are friends, co-workers, colleagues, or whether they just met. I try to do it all the time, even if I don't really need to, like at malls, or when I am out at a restaurant with friends. I like to know what is going on in the room that I am in, with the people that are in it, and since I can't, and wouldn't go around the room and ask people those things, or how they are, I rely on body language to give me a survey of the room. When you become excellent at reading body language, it becomes natural, and it gives you an instantaneous advantage over every single person in the room. I like having the advantage. You are reading this book because you want to have the advantage. All of our books are designed to give you that advantage.

Sweet Feet

The first thing I look at when I walk into a room is feet. Yep, feet. Stinky weird looking feet. Have you ever taken a look at a foot? They are fricken weird looking. Some people really like feet, which is fine, but that also makes you weird, because feet are enclosed in shoes all day, sweating and being sweaty, or they are out walking, encountering all the crap on the ground wherever they go. Feet aren't really meant to be "beautiful," they are meant to be practical. Keep that it mind. Feet are practical.

Feet are also the farthest part of the body from the brain. I went to one of those crazy exhibits once where they have people skinned and dipped in plastic so you can see all their muscles and bones. One of the displays was the nervous system. As I told you before, I have a deep love for brains, and all things related, such as nerves, and the system that they make. You could see the "wiring" of the human body going all the way down to the toes, and the feet are, indeed, the farthest thing from the brain. That means the impulses take a relatively long time to get from the brain to the feet. So feet don't react as quickly as things like hands or faces, which are close to the brain, so feet are relatively "hard wired."

So, feet are easy to read, because they don't get as much attention as body parts that are closer to the brain. An idea that you can remember, the farther you are from the brain, the more honest you get. Because of this, it is easier to lie with the face and hands, than it is the feet. Feet simply point to what the person likes, and away from the things he doesn't. Moving feet (bobbing up and down, for instance), is an indication of a happy person, whereas frozen, unmoving feet might be a sign that someone is nervous or doesn't like something or someone, especially if the feet were moving, then all of a sudden they "froze," like we talked about earlier.

So when I walk into any environment I look down at people's feet. If a girl is into a guy she is talking to, her feet will be pointed at him. If she isn't and wants to get out of there, her feet will be pointing away. If there are three people talking in a triangle, all the feet will be pointed toward the most important, interesting, or attractive person.

In the image, note the feet pointed away indicate lack of interest. She is about to make a run for it.

Feet pointing at you, or someone, is a sign of interest.

If a girl is sitting in a chair, and has her feet intertwined, she might be shy or nervous. If a man is sitting in a chair with his legs prominently crossed, he may not be listening to what the other person is saying (since he is forming a barrier with his feet). People who have just met for the first time may be standing with their feet crossed, one over the other. Feet, feet, feet. They rarely lie. They are hard wired.

If you are interested in meeting women, it is really easy to tell which ones are open, and which ones are shy. You need to change your approach accordingly.

This girl may be a little harder to approach as she appears to be closed off, upset, and/or bored. An approach is still (and always) possible; however you may have a higher level of difficulty.

The next thing I do is look at their belly button. Janine Driver, in her book called You Say More than you Think, calls this "naval intelligence." Belly buttons are a lot like feet; they don't get much direct attention from the brain, so they point to what they want, and away from what they don't.

Her feet and belly button are pointed away, so she may not be too interested in what is going on.

Arms, Chest, and "Private Parts"

So much for the easy to read stuff! As we move up the body, things get a little tougher to read, since the closer to the brain we get, the more conscious attention body parts get. Let's talk briefly about hands and arms. Sometimes people get cold. This is, of course, seen as a negative input to the brain, so it kicks into survival mode, and people cross their arms over their chest, and warm their fingers in the little ovens known as your arm pits. So, people might be cold. But another reason they may be protecting "vital organs," such as their hearts, lungs, or the lovely spleen, is that they are uncomfortable with what is going on or being said.

So at this point, let me take a break from things and tell you that you cannot read one particular piece of body language and get the whole story about someone. You have to read all the signs together to get the whole picture. So, if someone is standing in a cold room with her arms crossed and laughing at the same time, it probably just means she is just cold. If she is standing in that same room with arms crossed and a scowl across her face, it may mean that she is in a craptacular mood, or doesn't like what is going on. So take all the things we are saying into context.

Protecting vital organs are a sign of discomfort. Both men and women do this in emotionally uncomfortable situations.

When people are nervous, don't like what is going on or being said, or are in a generally bad mood, they will protect their chest and vital organs. This is just the back of the brain doing what it is supposed to, and helping you survive, in this case from a bad thought, or negative words. This also holds true for your private parts. Go to a funeral and look how people are standing at that funeral. Most people will have their hands over their private parts. That is because they are uncomfortable, or sad, and they are protecting themselves. No matter what vital organ they are protecting, if they are protecting it, you can guess that they are uncomfortable about something, closed off, and probably won't listen to much of what you have to say. They may also be harder to approach.

All of this is part of the "freeze" and "flight" parts of the limbic system we talked about earlier. When people are crossing things over vital bodily organs, you will notice they are not moving much (freeze), and also are hiding their vital organs from begin damaged (flight). This is the same reaction to negative activity, or even negative thoughts. So, if you want to pick the angry girl in a bad mood out of the room, look at the girl with her legs crossed, arms over her chest, with the mean look on her face. Don't approach her, unless you need to practice getting rid of some approach anxiety.

People who are in good moods, or are encountering or thinking about things that they like, will have the opposite reactions. They will open their arms, move around a lot, and generally look open and animated. If you see a group of people like this, they are likely in good moods. Especially if you are talking to a girl and she has that open posture.

This is a girl who is protecting her vital organs with her arms. She is pretty closed off.

The key, by the way, when dealing with people that have closed body language, is to get them to open up. Even if they are just cold, closed body language equals a closed mind, so if you want someone to listen to you, try to open them up somehow. The best way I have found is to hand them something to hold, like a drink, or your coat, or some kind of animal like a cat or chinchilla, if you have a spare chinchilla to give. I always carry at least two. You can also open your body language significantly in the hopes that her brain's mirror neurons decide to mimic you and your openness (it does happen).

A final note about hands and arms: when people are nervous, lying, uncomfortable, etc., they will try to pacify themselves. Think about having a cat that just got scared. You will try to calm that cat down by petting it softly on the head until it purrs. Incidentally, this works with girlfriends, too.

People do this to themselves when they are nervous, scared, or uncomfortable. They will do what is called "pacifying moves." They will "pet" their arms, rub the back of their heads, or run their hands nervously through their hair. All of these "pacifying moves" are designed to slow the heart-rate down, and create comfort. So, if you see someone "petting" themselves, rubbing their hands or arms together, or rubbing the back of their head, they may, for some reason, be uncomfortable. Or, they may think they are a cat or dog. If you friend that type of person, it could be really fun, or really creepy. Or both. A few years ago I watched an interview with a sexual predator on TV, and the moment he spoke about getting caught, he started patting the back of his head, which indicated that getting caught upset him.

Specifically for women, a common pacifying move is covering the "suprasternal notch." That is the little "hole" just below your neck and above your chest. Think about where a lot of women have their necklaces resting on their chest, the notch is usually right above that. It is right below your Adam's apple. When women are uncomfortable with something, they will cover this little notch with their hands, or play with a necklace just above it. It is a sign of "flight," as they are protecting a vulnerable part of their body. Men will do this too, by the way, but not nearly as much. You have probably seen this in men wearing ties. They will grasp or adjust the knot part of their ties when they get bothered. Guess what? The knot is right above the suprasternal notch!

She does NOT like what is going on... this could mean a lot of things, but primarily that something is making her uncomfortable, confused, or upset. Her face indicates this as well.

The Face

Out of all the body parts that we have covered, the face is the hardest to read. We can lie more easily with our face, but all the same rules apply as above. If a person is smiling while they are talking, and suddenly they stop and their face freezes, something has kicked off the survival part of the back of the brain. People make tiny little gestures in their faces when they encounter different kinds of information, which last for a half a second. These "micro gestures," are often hard to catch (although women are very adept at catching them), because we can cover them and make a new face depending on how we want to react.

For instance, if we hear a dumb joke that is not funny, we will frown for a half a second, before flashing a "fake" smile. If you practice reading faces of people, you will start to pick up on these micro gestures. We all make them, and they betray our true emotions, positive or negative, about any given experience, but quickly disappear because our conscious minds (the front parts of the brain) take over.

Still, faces can be a great way to read someone if you learn how to do it. The only thing we will address here in detail will be smiles. There are two types of smiles, real smiles, and fake smiles. We have all done one or the other at some time in our lives, like when someone tells a dumb joke and we want to be nice so we fake smile at them so that they will stop telling dumb jokes. Women will often fake smile just to be nice, but there is a way to tell the difference.

Real smiles, when people are really laughing, or are generally pleased by what is going on are easy to identify. When a person is smiling for real, the part of the face beside the eyes will crinkle up. This is where people get "laugh lines" or "crow's feet" outside of their eyes. There is a name for that muscle around the eyes, but who really cares? You can Google it. Fake smiles, that is, smiles that are meant to be polite but not convey real pleasure, do not crinkle up the eyes. So if people are just being polite, they will smile with their mouth only, and if people like what is being said, they will smile with their whole face, mouth and eyes. This is really helpful when you are trying to gauge if a girl is into you or likes what you are saying.

Which one of these is a "real" smile? The key to telling is if the eyes scrunch up.

We really haven't addressed "fighting" body language, which is important to know when trying to determine whether a man in the room might be hostile, but for brevity's sake, if he looks like he is waiting to punch someone, or fling his poo, just stay away from him. Gamma Males are often looking for a good fight, simply because they are Gamma Males. If you like a girl who is in a mixed group (men and women), this is an important thing to gauge before you make and approach. Avoid guys that look extremely closed, angry, aggressive, or hopped up on steroids, and the women with them.

Clothing

Before we move on to more specific body language cues of availability, it is important that we talk about clothing. There was a professor I had in college that used to say "clothing doesn't make the man, but it marks the man."

This is absolutely true, but clothing has a different purpose whether you are talking about men or women. Clothing is very important to understanding who a person is, where they come from, their value, as well as their respect of themselves.

Men

When it comes to men, clothing communicates social value, i.e. a man's social status. Looks aren't as important to women as they are to men, but social status is. A man's clothing conveys whether he is a successful CEO or an out-of-work burger flipper. However, even an out-of-shape guy or unsuccessful guy can communicate high social value if he wears the right clothes. Ripped, faded clothes, unkempt hair, and dirty, old shoes, communicate that a guy doesn't value himself, and neither should you value him very highly either (unless you are a famous rock star and this is your "style," but that is rare). Think about a guy wearing clothes that are fresh and bright, clean and kempt, a guy that looks "put together." This is the guy that you want to talk to and get to know, because his clothing communicates his high value.

We are not going to go into fashion styles for men here, because that is another book, but what we can say is that a guy should dress his age, and wear things that make him look good. You definitely need a woman's opinion on this! Don't trust your own judgment just because you *think* you look good in that old shirt of yours. Throw out the old stuff, or don't wear it unless you are fishing. Go with crisp, clean, lines that make you look good, and make you feel confident. I know that when I put on my Armani suit, I feel like a million bucks, and people treat me like I am worth millions.

So should you spend a lot of money on clothes? You should spend enough to make it look like you are trying. So yes. Buy a new shirt a month, and throw an old one out (or give it away). Have a couple of pairs of jeans and a nice blazer.

While I mentioned the Armani suit, I make sure that even if I buy a shirt at the mall, it fits me, is age-appropriate, matches my personality, and is easy to clean (dry cleaning means that it is probably going to be dirty most of the time!) Have a rotation of clothes that you wear when you go out. Have an outfit for a professional setting, and one for more casual affairs, but you still want to look "put together" even when you are casual. The nice thing is that men have things lot easier when it comes to fashion, because unlike women, we can get away with consistently wearing black jeans, and changing the shirt for variety. Still, women have a much better fashion sense, so always get a woman's opinion on what you are wearing. If your female friend doesn't like it, neither will most other women.

Let me briefly address "peacocking." Peacocking is basically wearing something outrageous to set yourself apart from the crowd and get attention. I think that looking "put together," is a much higher demonstration of your personal value than being goofy or by peacocking. Women want a stable and successful guy in the long term, and I am not sure that peacocking, that is, wearing goofy hats or doing outrageous things in order to draw attention to yourself, is always the best approach, especially if you don't have the personality to pull off your outrageous outfit or accessory. The best way to "peacock" is to look your best, and operate with unfailing confidence. It is more genuine anyway. If peacocking got you the girl, you will feel pressure to continually ramp that kind of thing up to absurdity. However, I will say, a well-placed, crazy item on your head will work to attract women, if you can pull it off. Unfortunately, most guys just look goofy doing that, and it is better to look good than be goofy.

<u>Women</u>

For women, clothing is a whole different matter. People build their lives on understanding how to dress women. Remember what we talked about before? Men are generally attracted to women that can reproduce. So long hair, bosoms, makeup and all sorts of other accessories help women communicate their fertility. Fertility is so important to us that whole cults and religions have been built around it. It is fertility that makes men and women immortal, so women use their clothing to communicate their fertility. They do this by making their breasts more pronounced, their hair longer (which we will talk about here in a bit), painting their nails, getting tans, wearing high heels to make their legs look longer (a sign of fertility), and a lot more.

Here is what you need to know about women and clothing: the more skin they show, the more fertile they are. Women, as you learned from high school biology class, have a monthly menstrual cycle. Without getting into too much detail, basically it takes about a month for all the conditions to be right in a woman's body for her to get pregnant. Once her body is ready, she has about three to four days when she can get pregnant, and then her body cleans itself out and prepares for this process to begin again.

This process requires a bunch of hormones, and makes women different from day-to-day depending on where they are in this cycle. Even if a woman is on artificial, chemical, birth control, this cycle still generally holds (however, there are many reports of a lowered sex drive in women on artificial birth control, since it basically tricks the woman's body into thinking it is pregnant).

During those three to four days of high fertility, a woman's temperature will rise slightly, and she will feel warmer than she does on other days. Thus, a woman who is the most fertile will show more skin and wear fewer clothes than normal. Also, nature has taken it upon herself to make them super horny during this time. Not that women don't want to have sex during those off times, but they are more likely to be physically active or even sexually active during high fertility days. We are programmed to procreate! It is how we survive.

Basically, a woman will use her clothing strategically, especially during times of fertility. She will choose her outfit based on its ability to both attract men and keep her cool. The difference between a highly fertile and less fertile is subtle, but with some training you can notice it. It is a lot less subtle in clubs and bars. Remember, we are wired to produce offspring. That goes for you too!

Chapter Twelve: Knowing The Easiest Girls to Approach

In the previous chapter, we talked about some quick tips on how to read the general body language of a room, and really, it applies to reading the body language of individuals. You have to read the room when you enter, so that you can determine the relationships there. Couples will generally be touching each other, while new relationships and co-workers will generally keep some distance. Figuring out who is most open, in the best moods, and who is having a good time will allow you to determine whom to approach. Girls that are looking to meet men should be standing or sitting in an open way.

But there are some more signals that should help you determine which girls are most open to being approached by a man. These signals are automatic, couched in the limbic system of the brain, and are therefore universal in nature.

Before we get to these signs, it is important to remind you about the nature of women that I mentioned early. When it comes to women, they almost all favor, in some way shape or form, passivity. That is because generally, female primates are smaller, slower, and physically weaker than male primates. Remember, they have to be more cautious about whom they approach because they can't go toe-to-toe with a male primate. So, they have to be passive, whereas the male is more assertive and direct. The passivity of females has helped them survive for millions of years.

Since women are much more passive than men, they expect men to be assertive, outgoing and confident. It is not a woman's job to actively approach a man she finds attractive; it is the man's job to approach her, and thus demonstrate his value as a confident and outgoing Alpha Male. So guys, if you are standing there at the club, beer over your chest (which is a sign that you lack confidence, but more on this later), waiting for the girl to approach you, you will be sadly disappointed. It is your job to approach her, and she will rarely, if ever, approach you, even if she really likes you. However, that doesn't mean the girl doesn't play her part.

One of my all-time favorite body language resources is called The Definitive Book of Body Language, by Allan and Barbara Pease. Get this excellent book, and keep it on your nightstand. The authors make an amazing statement which I agree with completely: 90% of approaches are *initiated* by the female. What?! Wait a minute, didn't I just say that it is the man's responsibility to approach, not the woman's? Am I smoking crack? How do these two things reconcile themselves?

Women initiate the approach by sending non-verbal signals, i.e. they express their interest in a man by their body language! They communicate to the room, and often to a specific man, that they are available. Men subconsciously pick this up, at least after a while, and the brave ones make the approach. It is the man's task to pick up these signals and make the approach. They can send these availability signals across the room, and if you see them, you will be able to pick out the easiest women in the room to approach. One of the problems that guys have is that they approach women that are not giving any signs of availability. Now that doesn't mean that you can't approach them, but it means that the approach has to be done differently, and you have a bit more difficulty (their perceived unavailability) to contend with.

So make it easy on yourself. Figure out which girls are making themselves available, and which ones aren't, and your night will go more smoothly. Sometimes, in a mixed group of women, you will get mixed signals too, which is to say some in the group are available and some aren't, such as married ones. Again, just because a woman is unavailable, or not making herself available, doesn't mean you can't approach; it just makes it a little more challenging to break through that barrier.

Signs of Availability

Women are very adept at reading body language, so they expect men to be with as well. But we aren't as good as they are, nor will we ever be, but with a little practice we can at least close the gap. This deficiency has cost many guys an easy approach, simply because a woman's signals of availability are subtle (there we go with that passivity stuff again), so subtle that men often completely miss what is going on. But not you, because you are about to get the inside scoop. So get your scooper ready.

To determine if a woman is available, the first thing you need to look at are her feet. If she is open, even with her legs crossed, her feet will be moving (if she is sitting in a chair). The bobbing up and down of her feet is a sign that she is in a good mood, but also, it is a call to attention. While I personally think that feet are kind of gross (as we have covered), women's feet are at least less gross than men's, and with their choice of shoe, they can dress them up and use them as a way to communicate.

Let's once again compare women to an animal. Think about a dog and its tail whipping around, saying to the room "pay attention to me!" The dog is sending a signal to the rest of the room that it wants attention, that it wants you to pet it. Women's feet are a lot like the dog's tail. They will whip them around, telling the room that they want the same thing, "give me attention, pet me, I want some dog food." Okay, do not give a girl dog food, because in this regard, they are not like dogs. Although it would be one heck of a funny opener if you could do it right.

When you see this going on, she is communicating to the room that she is available. The only time this does not apply is if she is already talking to a dude. In that case, her feet are moving because she is into the dude, which means that may not be an easy approach. But if several women are sitting together, whipping their "tails" (i.e. feet) around, they want some attention.

The next thing they will do, similar to the feet movement, is to whip their hair around. The same basic thing is happening, they are showing their fertility (by showing healthy hair), and also, it serves as another tail to flail to the room showing her need for attention. We will revisit this hair stuff in the next chapter. Another reason she is flipping her hair is to show her neck. A woman's neck is very vulnerable, and since we like survival, if she is protecting her neck (by covering that suprasternal notch we talked about in the last chapter) she is nervous. But if she is showing her neck, thus making herself (passively) vulnerable, she is communicating that she is making herself vulnerable to an approach from a dude.

Hair flip, showing healthy (and fertile) hair, and making her neck vulnerable.

In a like manner, a woman can "flail her tail" in a third way, and that is by showing her wrist. When a girl is flinging her arms around talking to friends (remember movement is a good thing, while "freezing" is a bad thing) showing her wrist has much of the same effect as showing the neck. It is a sign of vulnerability, essentially saying, "I am making myself vulnerable to an approach, and putting my defenses down."

Showing the wrist: another sign of vulnerability.

Two more things, and we will explain how to determine if she is specifically interested in you. First, a girl will laugh very loudly to make herself available to people in the room. Yep, we still do mating calls. Especially if there is a group of girls sitting and talking, the louder and more high-pitched they get, the more they are sending out the signal that they are available. Think about life in the forest. If you are scared, you don't make a peep, but if you are available to mate, you let the jungle know by some well-placed, high pitched grunts. In the <u>Odyssey,</u> the ancient Greek Epic, the sirens seduce the sailors by the sound of their voices, and then eat them. Remember this well, young Odysseus.

Feet. Check. Belly Button. Check. Hair. Check. Laughing and Smiling. Check.

Second, and this is so cool because it happens all the time, is something we call a "proximity alert." Despite their passivity, women get attracted to men too, and can make themselves available another way: by standing next to men. When a female primate (including a human one) is attracted to an Alpha Male, she can't just approach him directly, because he is bigger and stronger than her, so she must approach passively. Instead, the female primate will stand near (i.e. in proximity) the male she is attracted to, and very close at that, *with her back to him*. That enables her to have a quick escape if he turns out to be dangerous, since she is pointed in the right direction. She will then get "itchy," and start scratching her hand, and running her fingers through her hair and showing her neck and wrists. Often, with humans, she will have a friend immediately in front of her tell her what the male is doing. She is giving you an open door. You generally just have to turn and start talking to her and she will respond well. It is a lot of fun when it happens! Women are passive, just like cats are passive, but both know how to get your attention!

Signs of Attraction

You now know what a woman will do when she is making herself available to the whole room. The type of room determines how big these signs of availability are. For instance, in a coffee shop, the movements will be more subtle, and in a club or bar, they will be more grandiose because there is a lot more competition in the room, as well as distractions.

We have to remember that women can become very interested in men, so sometimes they get more specific than just sending out general "availability" signals. Sometimes they send out specific Signs of Attraction (SOAs). Remember, that by "attractive," we mean drawing everybody, not just women, into your reality. You should be attractive to friends, employers, and anybody else that you encounter. At The Joe Alpha Factor, we also emphasize that being attractive is a choice, not something that just magically happens, and so we keep attraction and being attractive at the center of our minds.

An SOA in this case is a direct signal that a girl is interested. In this context, a woman can send an SOA across the room to a specific guy, signaling him to come over and engage her. Sometimes women are really subtle with these SOAs and men miss the point, but sometimes, women are super-duper obvious about it, and flash a giant neon sign over their head. Some dudes are dumb enough to miss the sign, or get crippled by approach anxiety.

An example of an SOA from across the room is the body scan. In fact, it is their favorite one. Men have tunnel vision, evolved for seeing long distances in a narrow scope, perfect for hunting game down field. So, when a man "checks out" a woman, he often gets caught, because he has to move his whole head to scan a woman's body. Women's vision evolved differently for different needs, such as watching the children running around while they make dinner. They have a wider, but generally shorter, field of vision than men.

So when they check out someone else (man or woman) they generally don't have to move their whole head, or even their eyes like a man does.

So an SOA that women give from across the room is an *obvious* body scan, where she looks at a man up and down, from head to foot. For them, this is a giant neon sign. But many men miss this because we are bad at picking up their signals. So, a woman may send several SOAs directly at a man like this, scanning his body, making eye contact (for just a second) and then looking away. There may even be a micro gesture of a smile there too.

By the way, if a woman is looking at you and you make eye contact, hold the eye contact until *she* looks away. She is testing your confidence, and the man that looks away is not a confident man. Go practice making and holding eye contact with women at a mall or something, just don't be creepy about it!

Again, women don't need to scan to check us out, so when she is being obvious about it, she is sending a giant SOA.

The SOA Mandate

We believe in a principle called the "SOA mandate." The SOA mandate states that if you are getting SOAs from a woman, you are *mandated* to approach her and talk to her, even if you aren't that interested. For one, it keeps your skills up for when you are interested. Second, Alpha Males are social, so socialize a little. Third she might be the woman of your dreams, or one of her friends might be! Remember, beautiful women have beautiful friends. There is nothing wrong with being friends with a girl. They can open all sorts of doors for you and give you a lot of clout socially. Finally, the SOA mandate is a way for you to get over your approach anxiety. Since you have studied the way males and females interact (by reading this book!), you know that an SOA is a sign she is interested in you, and pretty much a sure sign at that. A Beta Male may pass up an SOA, but an Alpha Male *never* passes up an easy opportunity to approach and meet a woman, so get off of your butt...it's a mandate, dude!

Attraction happens at the subconscious level, so a girl may not even know she is sending you an attraction signal. Women are even "passive" when it comes to themselves! When you get an SOA, you have to move quickly so that approach anxiety doesn't kick in, and you get paralyzed. Even if she is with a guy, if she is attracted to you, there is a good chance she isn't attracted to him. Remember, go with your gut on these things, and don't overthink it! Her signals are subconscious, so learn to trust your subconscious!

So, if you are getting SOAs from someone, especially specific ones, go and talk to her. It is a mandate, which means that as an Alpha Male, you pretty much have to. Again, even if you aren't that interested, approaching like this keeps you geared up and in practice for when you are. When you become an Alpha Male, though, you will notice the SOAs shooting through the roof, which will, in turn, make more women attracted to you!

Chapter Thirteen: Physical Signs that She is Attracted to You

Let's assume you have made a successful approach. You saw the signs of availability that a girl has sent out to the room, or the specific Signs of Attraction (SOA's) that she sent your direction indicating an invitation to approach, and you are talking to her. How do you know how you are doing?

Her body language will help you gauge your success. One of the reasons that you need to have prepared "conversations," also known as routines, is so that you don't have to think too hard about what you are saying to her, so you pay attention to her body language, and her receptivity to you and what you are saying. It also helps you to be conscious of your own body language.

Let's go back to basics again for a moment. Our brains are hard wired to point toward what we want, and away from what we don't. Our reaction to negative input, either from the outside world, or our own thoughts, will cause us to react in three ways: freeze, flight, or fight. Our reaction to positive input will be the opposite; we will point toward it, exhibit open body posture, and be physically animated, moving feet, arms, hands, and having animated facial expressions. Also, we will naturally move toward what we want.

Let's revisit human nature for a minute. Our brains are wired the way that they are because of one reason, which is survival. Over the millions of years it took our brains to evolve, the people that were wired to survive, did, and passed that survival wiring down to their children, who passed it on. Survival is hard wired into our brains, to moving toward what makes us survive, and away from what doesn't.

Since our brains are wired for negativity, that is we are wired to detect what might kill us first, when we meet someone new, the automatic suspicion is that the new person is a foe, or an enemy, unless proven otherwise. Especially if that person is in clown makeup. Just expect that they are plotting some way to kill you and steal your soul. It is what clowns, and to a lesser extent, mimes, exist to do.

So our brains err on the side of caution, rather than expecting good out of people. Caution has helped us to survive. So, whenever you approach someone, you may get an automatic negative response from them. Don't take it personally; it is merely their brain doing what their brains do best. That means that when you approach a girl, you may initially get a "freeze" reaction, even if your approach was a good one. She is freezing because her brain is trying to figure out if you are friend or foe. So your body language in the approach needs to convey friendship, and at the very least be non-threatening.

Ever been shot down? I am assuming that you have at least approached one girl in your life, and if you haven't, let me tell you how most women shoot you down, or more accurately, how most men shoot themselves down. Most women, when you approach them, will freeze for a second. This is how most guys get "shot down," too. Most women will just stare at them looking frozen, because their limbic systems tell them to. That doesn't mean all is lost, but it does mean that you have to prove yourself to be a friend, and not a foe. We always default on the side of "foe." So expect, in a lot of approaches to get this "cold shoulder." It isn't that they are mean, but they like surviving as much as you do, and again, women have to be cautious. Most women will not run away (flight) or scratch your eyes out or be mean (although there are always a few like that). Most will just look at you funny (deer in the headlights) which is where it is vital to prove yourself as a "friend," which means you are not a threat to their physical, mental, or emotional survival.

So don't eject if you get the freeze reaction. Just be calm about it, and prove that you can provide them with both "safety and security," which is the primary thing on their minds. There are ways to minimize her negative reaction, using your own body language and the way that you approach her and her group.

When should you eject? Basically, whenever you get the perpetual cold shoulder from her. If you attempt to start a conversation and nothing *ever* happens, just walk away. Also, if your approach was successful, but the conversation goes sour, try to revive it, but if that doesn't work, then it is time to eject. If a girl is not interested, she isn't interested. Don't waste your time on girls that are clearly uninterested in you. Spend time on the girls that are. When that lack of interest is crystal clear, it is time to hit the eject button.

Now, let us assume that you have gotten past this initial "freeze out," and have proven yourself to be a "friend," and not a "foe." You have said the right things to prove not only are you safe and secure for her, but that you are a man of value, again, something you can communicate with your body language. How do you know if what you are saying is hitting the mark?

Well, you already have the tools at your disposal. If you are talking to a girl, and she is animated, that is, she is moving her feet, flailing her arms about, aiming her belly button toward you, making eye contact, etc., that means she is attracted to you enough to talk to you. She will laugh at your jokes, even if they are dumb, and her laugh will be boisterous and loud.

She will also give you further signs of availability, such as showing her neck and wrist, and pushing her hair around. Hair is their best sign! Again, think of a dog's tail. If it is flailing about, it means it is happy, and just keep petting it that way and the tail will keep moving. Pet it the wrong way, and the tail will stop moving. Men are primarily attracted to signs of fertility in a woman, and when she is flipping her hair around, she is not only telling you she is available, but that with her long and healthy hair, she is fertile.

As we mentioned above, the brain directs the body to move toward what it likes, which means that if she is attracted to you, she will move toward you. She will put herself more physically in your space, and begin to touch you. Touching you is a huge SOA. If she touches you, that is a major sign that she is into you and attracted to you. The more she touches you, the more she is attracted to you. If she touches you, then touch her back, but keep it at the same level, at least publicly. We will talk about you touching her in the next chapter.

Your goal at this point is to make her feel comfortable around you (safe and secure), and make her more attracted to you. Eventually, the girl you want to attract will start ignoring her friends, and give all of her attention to you, at which case you can move her away from her friends, if it is appropriate.

Another sign that she is attracted to you is if she begins to "clean" and "groom" you. Think of the monkeys again. When they groom each other, it is a sign of their affection. If a girl straightens your tie, or picks the lint off of your shirt (even if there isn't lint, she will still pick it off), it is a sign that she is into you. We are all still primates you know! One little trick to see if a girl is attracted to you is to place a little lint on your shoulder, or purposefully make your tie crooked. Interested women will be sure to "groom" you and make sure you look put-together again.

So, what happens if you mess up? Well, again, you already know the answer if you have read this book. If she becomes uninterested, she will stop moving her hands and feet, she may cross her legs, and she will face away from you. She will stop touching you, and she will stop sending you the signs of availability, like moving her hair, and showing you her neck and wrists. She may also start doing some pacifying behaviors, such as covering the suprasternal notch, or "petting herself on the back of the neck or head." She may also ignore you. Don't worry! All is not lost at this point, unless you just told her she is fat, dumb, or ugly. That tends to end conversations!

If you went too far touching her, or said something that got her angry, or even showed too much attraction to her, she may back off. Backing off doesn't mean you are done, but you need to counter that with your own body language which we will address in the next chapter. If she is doing this, you have set off the "survival" part of her brain, and you need to once again prove that you are a high value "friend" (i.e. safe and secure). Many things can set off the survival part of their brains, and as long as you didn't do the "fat, dumb, and ugly" comment, or grab her inappropriately, the situation is salvageable.

She does not like this touching. You can see the "flight" response. This dude must have been acting quite the Gamma Male to get this response!

You need to be keenly aware of her body language at all times, because she is going to say more with her body than her words. And what is more important than her words, at least vocally, is the tone of her voice. Grunts and pointing! It all goes back to this!

I promise you, that she is keenly aware of your body language. If this book has taught you anything, it is that women are body language reading machines!

In the next chapter, we will talk about using your own body language to your advantage in any given situation, including entering a room, approaching the girl, and controlling your interactions with a female in conversation.

Chapter Fourteen: Attractive Body Language

We have made a giant assumption here. That assumption is that you are a human being. If you are not a human being, you can stop reading here because you can just abduct people and do your experiments on them. If you are a human, and not some kind of zombie or space monster, then you have a human brain too! That means all of this body language stuff applies to you as well. You are communicating all sorts of things through your body language. That means that you need to become aware of what your body language is expressing. Many people are unaware of what their body language is communicating, which is actually an advantage for you in two ways. First, it is easier to read them because they aren't overriding their honest body language. Second, by focusing on your own body language, you can more accurately communicate with your body, and keep your cards close to your chest. Both of these give you an advantage when dealing with anyone, not just women.

I have mentioned previously that women evolved their keen ability to learn body language in order to attract the best mates. Further, women stayed in the village while the males were out hunting, and thus spent more time relating to one another and to the kids. Thus, they developed these profound skills of reading body language, which is the source of "women's intuition." The intuition comes from the fact that they can read micro gestures in the face, and pick up body language better, because they had to, in order to survive and relate. So, you have to be especially aware of what you are communicating to women, because they are intuitively watching body language. The following sections will give you some helpful tips to utilize your body language to convey confidence and poise, and to be attractive to everyone, man, woman, and child.

How to Enter a Room

You begin the moment you enter the room. When you enter the room you have to keep something in mind, conscious or subconsciously, people are watching you. The way you enter the room determines how you will later interact with that room. If you enter timidly, people will notice this, and it will reflect badly on you. The body language of your approach is especially important when entering a loud and noisy room, like a bar or club, since hearing is difficult and people must analyze your body language to size you up. Keep this in mind whenever you enter any room, any time of the day, whether it is your classroom, office, bar, club, or even church. People are social by nature, and they are constantly and subconsciously making assessments of everyone in the room. They have to do this, because their brains are wired for survival, so they are constantly sizing everyone up as friend or foe, even if unconsciously. You do it too.

How you enter the room is determined by what you do before you enter the room. If you read the section on approach anxiety, we mention the "testosterone instaboost." This is the scientifically proven concept that holding confident poses increases testosterone levels. In this way, your thinking shapes your posture (e.g. if you are thinking depressing thoughts, you will have depressing body language), and the reverse is true: your posture and body positioning affects your mental state.

So, before you even enter a room, you should be practicing positive, confident body posture, and you will feel more positive and confident.

When you enter a room, know that everyone is either consciously or subconsciously assessing you. If you enter confidently, they will judge you as confident and will treat you with respect. If you enter like you are afraid, they will treat you the same way. No woman, boss, etc., wants to interact with a scaredy-cat. Nobody does.

So enter the room like you own the room. Seriously, imagine what it would be like to own the place, and act like that! Enter with your head up, your arms at your side in an open posture, and walk with purpose, like you have somewhere to be, because, dammit, you are an important guy. If you radiate importance, people will treat you with importance. It will register in the minds of all in the room that you are an Alpha Male. Women are attracted to Alpha Males. Heck, men are attracted to them too, and will become your followers.

Let's think of a model for this behavior. How do you think Donald Trump enters the room? Shoulders down, looking down at the ground? Heck no! He enters the room, every room, as if he owns the room, and you know what? I bet he *does* own every room he walks into. And if he doesn't have the deed to the room, I guarantee anybody watching him thinks he owns it.

Own Your Space

That brings us to our next principle, the "Alpha Executive." Trump is an Alpha Executive in two senses. First, he enters any room "as if" he owns it, and, in a sense, for that moment, he does "own" the room because he is the Alpha Male there. Second, when he gets to where he is going, his desk, seat, or his table at a restaurant, he "owns his space." He doesn't sit closed off, and afraid. He sits confidently, taking up as much space as possible in a normal way. Taking up space is a way to mark territory.

The Alpha Male owning his space

Watch Trump on his Television show, "The Apprentice." The man owns the board room, and takes up the most space of anyone in the room. So, if you are standing at a table, sitting at a desk, eating at a restaurant, always communicate the ownership of your space to everyone in the room. It is what a good Alpha Male does.

Do this with open and confident posture, with your head up. Even if there are more important people, and bigger Alpha Males than you present, you are still the owner of your own territory, so act like it.

This is very important, especially if you are in a club. Do not cross your arms over your chest. In fact, don't put anything over your chest, as it is a sign that you lack confidence. As we said above, when we are nervous or uncomfortable, or feeling cold, our natural instinct is to cover our vital organs to protect them. However, confident people, especially people who are comfortable being in the public eye, never do this. Confident people always portray themselves as confident, and when you leave your chest exposed, that is you don't cover it with your arms, you are saying to everyone around you, "I am so confident that I am leaving my vital organs exposed... go ahead and attack me."

Of course, you are not literally inviting an attack, but subconsciously, you are saying that you are afraid of nothing. An even more extreme version of this is to stand with your hand clasped behind your back, exposing your chest even more. Think for a second about how a soldier or a police officer stands "at ease." "At ease" for these guys is feet shoulder width apart, with hands clasped behind their back. They are so "at ease" that they can expose the whole front part of themselves: chest, private parts, and all. That is why it portrays confidence. This stance actually can come off as a bit aggressive, so you don't want to stand in the club like a security guard, as it can push you into the "foe" category we talked about before. Do look at the bouncer next time you go into a club, though. I bet he will be standing this way.

Guys cover their chests all the time in a club or bar (or anywhere for the matter). That is probably because they are feeling approach anxiety. In these settings, most men cover their chest by holding their drink right in front of their chest. Notice it next time you go out. It is a very common sign of insecurity. It is the same thing as crossing your arms, and covering your chest, except with your drink.

This guy is using a cup to cover his chest, a sign of insecurity. Note her lack of interest.

Look around the bar again, and see that the super confident dudes aren't doing that at all. Usually, their drink is by their side, exposing their chest in all its "come mess with me and see what happens" glory. Those are the Alpha Males. Those are the guys who attract women, and then meet them.

Nothing over the chest.... she likes this!

The Body Language of Approaching a Group

In this section, we are not going to cover what to *say* when you approach a group. That is for Part IV. This chapter deals with body language, and body language alone. That being said, if you are going to be a successful Alpha Male, you need things to say. It doesn't matter if you are meeting a group of women, a group of managers at the mixer, or the cashier at the drug store, always have some "material" in reserve.

Routines will be covered more extensively in Part IV, but in regards to body language, having pre-prepared material lets you focus your mental energy and attention on things like body language, because you are not always having to think about what to say next. Routines should flow into regular, comfortable conversation, and exist to help you restart conversations if they get stale. Again, if you have material that you are comfortable with, something you can talk to everyone about, then you can focus your energy on things like your body language and theirs, and also appear calm, confident, and approachable.

Before we talk about how to approach a group, let us review what is going on in people's brains. Everyone is wired for survival. If you survive, you pass on your genes. Remember, whenever someone meets another person for the first time, each is sizing the other up, either as a friend or enemy. That is why the body language of people who have just met starts off closed, but gradually opens up. Remember too, that our default setting when meeting new people is to view them as "foe" first, and "friend" later. There are many evolutionary reasons for this. One reason is that in the jungle, everyone competes for resources, so anyone not in your "tribe" is competition, and therefore a "foe."

When people first meet, each has to prove himself as a "friend." This is why first impressions are so important. They are the impressions that stick. So, your body language at the very least needs to reflect that you are not a "foe."

Your approach to a group will communicate this. If you walk up to a group directly, at a fast pace, how do you think they will react? Even though you may not intend to be overwhelming in your approach, often when people are nervous, they move rapidly and awkwardly, giving the appearance of being threatening. Remember the cat from Chapter Two? He did not react well to a direct approach. I should note that I have attempted, and have been successful with, a direct approach, so I know it can be done, but I would not recommend it for most approaches, for the reasons I have illustrated above.

The Direct Approach...not always a good idea. Note how threatening it looks!

Women are a lot like cats. How would you approach a cat? If you approach a cat directly, most of them will turn and run. So with cats, and women, you have to be indirect and somewhat passive in your approach. You don't want to spook her, because once a girl sees you as a threat, in any way shape or form, you have lost her. Safety and security are always on their minds.

Therefore your approach should be indirect. You should walk as if you are going to pass her by, as if speaking to her is almost an afterthought. Your body direction shouldn't be pointed directly at her, as she may see that as a threat. The best way to approach a cat, and a woman, is to sachet beside them, and make them feel comfortable. Basically, you casually walk beside her, slightly passing her by, and then turn back slightly and engage her, with your feet pointed a different direction. Do you see how completely non-threatening this is? Then, if she lets you into their "tribe" by engaging you, you can face your body toward her. Check her body language as we described in the proceeding chapters to see if she is comfortable. This reduces the "freeze" response, and frames you as a "friend," rather than a "foe."

The Indirect Approach... she is almost an afterthought...

When you are approaching in lower key environments, such as coffee shops, these rules apply as well, but your approach should be even subtler. If you are sitting in a chair near her, you shouldn't face her to open her up. Instead, turn your head and speak over your shoulder. Make sure you learn this principle: indirect is non-threatening.

False Time Constraint

Let's say you are a young primate male wandering through the forest, and you come up to a new tribe. You are not part of that tribe yet, and so you are seen as a "foe," someone who is trying to steal women and food from the tribe. While they don't attack you right away, since your approach was cautious, the tribe looks at you and wonders two things: What do you want? How long are you going to be here?

Tribalism is alive and well, and people are still suspicious of new people who come close to their tribe. To allay these suspicions, you must communicate verbally, as well as non-verbally, that you will not be staying long. How do you do this? The answer has really been given already. Can you guess? Point your feet and belly button in the direction that indicates that you are ready to leave. Even though they likely won't be body language experts, they will still know what that means, because we all know what it looks like when someone is leaving.

At that point, if you have demonstrated yourself as a potentially valuable friend, the "Law of Scarcity," as seen in Robert Cialdini's book <u>Influence</u>, will kick in. The Law of Scarcity comes from our evolutionary background as well. Basically, when a resource is scarce, or can potentially be lost (such as a potentially valuable friend being able to walk away), humans perceive that person or thing as being more valuable. The false time constraint accomplishes two things. First, you are showing yourself to be "scarce," and therefore more valuable. Second, you are showing yourself to be confidently detached, which is the opposite of "needy." Women hate needy. Heck, everyone hates needy. Needy people are just a burden to your survival. Why? From an evolutionary standpoint, needy people need more care, and use a lot of the tribe's time and resources, which makes survival harder.

He has somewhere else to be, and it shows

Touching

Touching is also a key part of body language. People who like each other touch each other. Parents hug their kids, friends pat each other on the back, and athletes smack each other on the butt, which, by the way, I never got, nor was comfortable with.

Touching is a good thing, as it shows connection and familiarity. When it comes to touching people you have just met, it is appropriate to touch them as long as it is natural. How would you touch your friends or family? At first you can touch a girl you just met like that. If you do not get a negative response, as indicated by reading her body language, you can touch a little more and a little more, until she show any signs of discomfort. If she does, simply take a couple of steps back, and let her be comfortable with you again. Then, slowly reintroduce touching.

Touching, especially women you might be romantically interested in, is a process. You never go from shaking hands with a girl to kissing her, unless you never want to see her again. You need to build up to that: touch her on the arm, then the hand, then put your arm around her, kiss her on the cheek, and finally, when the time is right, on the lips. If you make touching a comfortable part of your relationships from the beginning, then it will feel natural when it is time for more intimate touching. When it comes to touching, be respectful of her, but also be confident. If you act sheepish, you will communicate fear and lack of confidence. If you go a little too far, too fast, she will certainly tell you. At that point all is not lost. Just back off to a point where she is comfortable, and start building that comfort in touching again. Just remember, safety and security are important to women, but they like to be touched! They love it! So, touch them, appropriately and confidently.

We once had a client who would not touch girls, caused in part by approach anxiety. He went on two or three dates with the girl. Once she even bought him a gift at the beginning of the third date! And then she didn't talk to him again. If a girl is attracted to you, and you notice a romantic spark, and you *don't* touch her, you will look afraid, and therefore like a low value Beta Male. Alpha Males are assertive in the way they touch (not aggressive), just like they are assertive in everything. A good way to firmly put yourself in the friend zone is not to touch a girl you are interested in. Touching is a very important part of relationship building.

If she touches you, and lets you touch her, she is interested. Touching is good!

Touching is good and normal if it is done naturally

Breaking Rapport

If you go too far too fast, or say something to tick her off, or you notice negative body language for one reason or another, punishment and reward is one solution that uses body language to reestablish a connection, and get them to chase you. It should also be used when things are going well, to make them chase you a little, and show yourself confident and detached, and therefore not "needy." Finally, I find that this is a good way to gauge a girl's interest in you.

The concept is simple. Break rapport with them. "Rapport," which we will treat more extensively in Part IV, is another word for "connection." Remember what we said in the first few chapters about belly buttons and feet? That they point to what they like and away from what they don't. Two people that are into each other will be pointing their feet and belly buttons at each other. To break rapport with her, simply turn your feet and belly button away from her. Do it without warning. Even mid-sentence. Point them toward the door, or toward another girl. Just move your whole body away from her by about 45 degrees.

If you have ticked her off and she is giving you negative body language (freeze, flight...if she is fighting you, then you are a real screw up) then simply do this technique, but don't leave. Or, if things are going well, just all of a sudden do this, and watch what happens.

Breaking Rapport

In either case, if she is attracted to you, she will try to reestablish rapport with you by getting back into your field of vision, by moving in front of your feet and belly button. I have seen this many times with our clients, not because they are in trouble, but to make the girl to chase them, and to test their attraction. By using this technique, they will chase! It is really a pretty cool thing to watch how quickly they will try to get back in front of you.

If you are in a mall together, simply walk away from her. This is another variation. She will come looking for you. I promise. It shows you are cool to leave her, and that you are not needy.

Here is the best part. Even if she didn't move herself in front of you after you turned away, when you turn back to her and "reward" her with your attention, she is going to like you more. So even if she didn't pass "breaking rapport" attraction test, guess what? The "Law of Scarcity" tells us that because you made yourself scarce for a moment, she will find you more attractive. That's right: you win either way!

Why does this work? Dr. Jeffrey Schwartz, in his book, <u>You Are Not Your Brain</u> cites a UCLA study led by Dr. Naomi Eisenburg on social rejection. In her experiments, participants played a virtual game of ball with two virtual players, controlled by the researchers. In the game they tossed the ball back and forth between the two virtual players, and the human player. Eventually, the two virtual players stopped tossing the ball to the human player, and only to each other, simulating social exclusion. The human player was also hooked up to a brain scan machine, which detected that when the person was socially excluded by the virtual players, the same part of the brain that lit up when *physical* pain was experienced lit up! Thus, socially exclusion actually causes physical pain.

"Breaking rapport" capitalizes on this part of our brain that reacts so poorly to exclusion. When exclusion happens, there is pain. When we return to paying attention again, there is a sensation of "reward," directly related to the ending of pain. When you "break rapport," and then "reward" them with your attention, you are ending the feeling of pain.

This makes perfect sense, for if we go back into our evolutionary history, to be excluded from the tribe meant death! We organize ourselves into social groups for a reason, and that reason, which is wired into our brains, is survival. Social groups help us survive, since people complement each other's skills, or lack thereof. So for us to be excluded is synonymous with death. No wonder our brains react so poorly to being excluded, as it works against our survival wiring, and this is why the punishment/reward strategy also works to strengthen our relationship with others and increase our value in their eyes.

The SOFTEN Technique

Now we are coming to the end of the body language section of this book. We can sum up a lot of your interaction with others with the SOFTEN technique. Alan Garner explains this technique in his book <u>Conversationally Speaking</u>. The SOFTEN technique is explained below.

1. Smile

Smiling denotes comfort, and comfort denotes confidence. If you are comfortable in your space, that means you are confident that nothing bother you. Smiling is an important part of communicating this fact.

You must be careful about smiling though, simply because you want to smile like an Alpha Male, and not a Beta Male. The "smiling Beta," is the guy with that cheesy look on his face because he wants people to like him, but too desperately. He is the guy who smiles too long at the girls, and looks generally goofy. He smiles to please others, and it is clear to everyone.

An Alpha doesn't have a big toothy grin on his face, but more of a slight smile which denotes confidence in his environment. It is a smile that says, "I am smiling because I own the damned place." It is almost a smirk or a one sided smile, where you are smiling with only one half of your mouth. This is the smile you need to have when you approach a group of people, and then stop smiling altogether, at least until someone says something of value. Then, your smile is their reward.

2. Open Posture

We have mentioned this frequently, but it is worth repeating. An open posture not only shows confidence, but demonstrates that you are open to social interaction.

3. Forward Lean

Leaning forward is a sign of interest, while leaning away shows you are uncomfortable with someone. Slightly leaning into someone when speaking to them shows you are interested in them, and that you are giving them your attention. If you want to show interest (to build rapport, "reward," etc.), then lean forward. If you want to show you don't care or are uninterested (to "punish" or show detachment), then lean away.

4. Touch

As I have mentioned, touch has gotten a bad rap, but when used ethically, touch demonstrates interest. Slight and non-offensive touching makes people like you. Cialdini suggests that even slightly brushing somebody (such slightly touching somebody when you receive change) can give them a more favorable opinion of you.

5. Eye Contact

Women are much better at making eye contact than men, and this holds true even for babies (baby girls hold eye contact much longer than baby boys). Eye contact demonstrates interest and confidence. Lack of eye contact shows weakness, hesitancy, and lack of interest.

6. Nod

Nodding indicates agreement and is a way to establish rapport. It is also effective in getting someone to agree to your point-of-view.

Perhaps the best lesson is: never...ever... ever be this needy

Chapter Fifteen: Final Thoughts on Body Language

A lot of Part III has been dedicated to reading body language in regards to meeting the woman of your dreams, but all of these things work with people in any situation. If you are meeting your boss for the first time, trying to make a sale, giving your parents bad news, or whatever communication you might be trying to make, remember that your body language will make communication easier or harder.

You also will be better able to understand where people are coming from when you are able to read their body language. If you are speaking publicly and need to gauge the crowd, their body language will tell you everything. If you are in an interview, you can determine which of your answers are impacting the interviewers, and you can answer them in a confident way.

If you are selling something, these body language techniques will also help you put confidence behind your product or service. Everything we do with people is about "selling." Whenever we interact with people, we are "selling" them ideas, to get them to go where we want them to go.

I have to say, learning how to read body language, and knowing how to change my own body language, provides me the advantage in almost every situation I enter. When you learn body language, it is as if you begin to read the minds of everybody you meet. Personally, I don't tell people I am a body language expert, because I find that when I tell them, they become guarded and distrustful. They think I am reading them all the time... which...I am! You will do this too! However, people get nervous and awkward when they know you can read them like a book, and they don't like to be at such a disadvantage.

Part IV: What to Say and How to Say It

Chapter Sixteen: Environments

The art of meeting people and forming relationships is just that, an art. So let's think about art here for a second. Have you ever seen that Bob Ross guy on PBS? He is that white dude with a 'fro from the 70's who quietly and gently painted pictures, in a way that seemed ever-so-soothing?

An artist has to work with many different mediums. He has to work with canvas, wax paper, clay, brick, and many others. The medium he uses will determine what tools he uses to produce his art. For instance, you wouldn't use water colors if you are going to paint a mural on a brick wall. A good artist adjusts his tools for the medium his is working with. Further, he must adjust his technique based on what he is painting on and with. Again, you can't paint with watercolors the same way you paint with acrylic. The technique will be different.

The same is true for meeting people, and especially women. You should be able to, with some practice, meet women whenever and wherever you are. You simply have to learn to adjust your technique and style based on where you find yourself. The dynamics of your approach anxiety may also change. You can't use a "shoot down set" in a coffee shop for instance, if the girl you meet is the only one there.

Coffee Shops (and Other Low Key Environments)

Approaching people in a coffee shop, mall, grocery store, or a general public place requires a softer touch. It requires you to be more subtle, and the SOAs that you receive from a girl will also be more subtle. You don't want to overpower her and make her feel unsafe. Remember, if you make a woman feel unsafe at any point in your conversation, she will never talk to you again. Your contact in these environments should be more casual, much more laid back, and very safe for you both. At the same time, you should exhibit a quiet confidence in your movements and body language. An Alpha Male *always* owns his environment, but some environments are easier to defend than others.

Approaches in coffee shops and malls are more difficult, simply because you have more "to lose." What I mean is that if you get shot down there, everyone in the place will easily see it, and your brain will make you think that you will get "kicked out of the tribe," or suffer social death. When approaching in low key environments, you have to use the techniques in the previous chapters to get over approach anxiety to help me realize that rejection does not equal death. Always remember that you can just walk out of the room.

Basically, environments that are not packed with people require more effort to overcome approach anxiety, as well as a softer, more subtle approach. In these areas, the approach can be done in a line, sitting near enough to someone to strike up a conversation, or a walking past someone, in a non-threatening way, with an appropriate question in mind, such as "what book is that?" or "where is that store that sells funny T-Shirts?" We will discuss opening conversations in the next chapter.

Clubs and Bars

Clubs and bars are a different situation altogether. They are loud. They are dark. They are usually full of people. You have a lot less to lose there (since the room is so big, a shoot down won't cost you as much), and the reactions, such as SOAs are going to be bigger and easier to notice, as the noise makes communication with body language more necessary. Your approaches can be a lot less subtle, and actually need to be a lot more lively here to compensate for the noise and distractions. Remember, confidence is communicated here primarily by body language.

You don't want to meet your future wife in a club. Well, maybe you will, but with the alcohol and the competition that you have to face (there are a lot of Gamma Males in bars) clubs are ideal, in my mind, for one thing: practice.

Bars and clubs are where you will find women, and if you find the right place, lots of them. It is where they go to meet people. But, the downside of clubs and bars is that all the women in there have their defenses up that we mentioned in previous chapters. Women at bars and clubs are indeed there to meet men, but they all know that those men generally just want to get into their pants. Their defenses are high... DefCon 5 high! You will have to do a lot of work to get them to even talk to you, which is good practice. Great practice in fact! And as we have covered before, everyone is practice.

So, clubs and bars provide a target-rich environment of women, but the trade-off is that they are a little harder to talk to. Alcohol is a good advantage for you though, not that you should be drinking, but since the women have likely been drinking, they should be easier to approach. We encourage our clients refrain from drinking alcohol in clubs or bars, or not drink that much. We are not against drinking - God knows we aren't - but you need to develop genuine confidence, not "liquid confidence," and you always want your wits about you, so you can meet people the best way you know how.

Clubs and bars are also full of Gamma Males, which is a problem. Gammas are normally angry types with low self-esteem, but get them drunk and they become even bigger jerks. They look to start fights, to defend what they perceive are their women, or just because they are jerks.

If you keep these points in mind about clubs and bars, you can remain detached, and have a good time practicing. You will get shot down a lot, which will immunize you in the long run from rejection. Everyone gets shot down; however, as time goes on and your skill increases, you will get shot down less and less.

Death on the Dance Floor

Do not, under *any* circumstances, try to meet girls on the dance floor, especially if you aren't good at dancing, which is just about every man. There is nothing but death waiting for you there. Women equate dancing with being good at sex, and being able to fight, so if you can't do it, then don't *ever* **ever** go on the dance floor. The only time I do it is to be funny, and it is a giant risk. It is funny because I am such a big guy, but I only do it if it is absolutely necessary. The girls there are usually dancing with other girls in what I call "The Circle of Death." They are there to dance, not to talk to you. Besides, it is loud, and you have to yell to be heard. Your chances of getting shot down go up exponentially on the dance floor. Wait until they go back to their table, and focus your attention on girls who are not dancing.

The dance floor is ALWAYS... ALWAYS a trap. You cannot own your space if you are flailing around on the dance floor looking like an idiot. By the way, next time you go to a club with a dance floor, notice something: it is usually a bunch of girls dancing, and a few dudes *trying* to dance. Surrounding the dance floor are a bunch of dudes hanging out with each other, or alone, holding their drinks at chest-level looking insecure, just hoping one of those girls will come up and start talking to him. That never happens by the way.

Do you see why this is pure death? Virtually no man "wins" in this situation!

The Ideal Environments to Meet Women

There are happy mediums between the subtle coffee shop/grocery store environments, and the clubs and bars (you should be able to meet people in *any* environment), and those are networking events and conventions.

Conventions and networking events are a nice mix of the low key environment and the intense environment of the bars and clubs. By networking event, I mean anything from a church social, to a business or social networking event set up by the chamber of commerce, young professionals group, or even a party thrown by friends.

Let's address conventions first. They have a lot of great things going for them. They are almost always high energy events. Conventions are all about new ideas, lots of people in a room, and an open crowd that allows you to make approaches safely and easily. Conventions are environments where people are primed to meet people. In fact people are there for that very reason, not only to get new ideas about their industry or cause, but also to meet people within that industry. That is the nice thing about conventions: you can go with virtually no knowledge of that particular subject and meet some nice attractive woman to educate you, and thus form a relationship. Your questions are genuine, as is the conversation. You don't even have to be that creative. You just talk about whatever the convention is about.

An even better option is going to a convention about a topic you are familiar with! In this case, you can be "excellent" in her presence as you demonstrate your knowledge about the topic, and it is an environment where you can be an Alpha Male! You can take that energy from the talks and the new people and the crowd, and parlay that into a one-on-one relationship that can continue immediately after the convention closes. The energy and the crowd (which creates a reduction in social risk that is found in coffee shops) will help you. Plus you have a reason to approach people, and that is the point of the convention!

Networking events are great too. As I mentioned above, networking events can be categorized as anything that is intended to create an environment where people can meet. Church socials, social clubs, networking events set up by networking companies for business, the chamber of commerce, and even parties thrown by friends. The reason that these are so great is that these environments are set up for people to meet people. These are places where approach anxiety should be minimized, simply because the environment is purposefully created to make approaching easier.

When The Joe Alpha Factor trains guys, we take them to Networking events first. It is a low pressure, easy way to meet people, with little or no approach anxiety. We instruct our clients to meet ten new people, get their information, and follow up with them later. We don't really care if they approach men or women, because the point is to habituate themselves to the art of meeting people. Whether it is a networking event, party, church social, social club, bar, club, coffee shop, or grocery store, the dynamic of approach, conversation, and establishment of rapport is essentially the same. It is the level of intensity that must be adjusted, depending on the environment. The little chart below breaks down the intensity level of different locations.

Intensity:

Coffee Shop: 1-3

Networking Event: 4-7

Club or Bar: 8-10

In all cases, regardless of intensity, you should demonstrate confidence, and be sure to always own the space in your environment.

Chapter Seventeen: Talk Dammit!

Whew! This has been a long journey so far, and before we go on, I think it is important to note something very important. You have to practice one thing at a time. You can't just read this book and decide that you are going to use body language, do an approach, try to get over your approach anxiety, be funny and interesting, and be excellent and gone, all in one setting.

As you have noticed throughout our book, we don't take the "change everything at once" approach. We will gladly train you, so if you are interested, let us know; it is far better than being trained by a book. We will create a program designed just for you, and help you address problems that you might be completely oblivious to. Visit joealpha.com for more information. We create change incrementally, one step at a time. We take you to a networking event so you can start off by just talking to people. Then, we take you to a club for the "shoot down" night, so that you learn how to overcome your approach anxiety. Next, we work with you to change your appearance and style, to look your best when you go out. We also have a session where we take clients to the mall to watch body language, and we point out what is going on. We also teach you about your mental inner game. And, of course, we go out with clients to public events, coffee shops, and festivals and work as their mentors and "wing-men." It is fun, exciting, and educational for our clients, and we find that they often change quickly and easily.

So, what we are saying is that this all takes time and focus. Focus on improving one thing at a time, and then after some time, trials, successes and failures, you will begin to weave it all together in your mind and through your actions. By doing this, you will start to become the Alpha Male that you want to be, and who men want to be, and women want to be around! Being an Alpha Male is really about learning these techniques and applying them, flexibly and detached, in all situations. There is another level beyond the Alpha Male. Many are content with being the Alpha, but we are never done learning and there is more: the "Theta Male."

All Theta Males are Alphas, but not all Alphas are Thetas. A Theta Male transcends mere "technique," and crosses over into deep understanding of why people, the universe, nature, work the way that they do. The Theta Male is on his way to perfecting that "inner game" that we talked about before. It is almost spirituality in a sense, where the Theta Male realizes the relationships between the past, present, and future. He understands the dynamics of reality, from quantum physics to the deepest recesses of human nature and the mind. He follows and influences social trends, and contemplates: he is mindful, he is present, and he is transcendent.

It would be impossible to encapsulate all that a Theta Male is into a book, even though we cover bits and pieces of it in this book, because a Theta Male is always learning and becoming a greater person. A technique, like those in this book, can be learned and perfected, but like in sports, the difference between a talented player and a professional athlete is what is happening in his mind, body, and spirit. If this intrigues you, then definitely contact us. We will make you an Alpha Male, but more importantly, we will give you the tools to create whatever reality you want, and attract anything into your life that you desire. This means leaving behind old ideas, and embarking into unknown territory of the universe.

OK! Back to the Alpha Male stuff! It turns out the women like to talk! Who would have thought!? In the book <u>Why Men Don't Listen and Women Can't Read Maps: How We're Different and What to Do About It</u>, Barbara and Allan Pease outline the differences in men and women. One of those many differences is that women have *three* times the language centers as men, and they process things more relationally and emotionally than linearly and spatially like men do. This happened, as we have mentioned before, through the process of evolution. Men went out for the hunt, not talking much, so as not to scare off the animals, and women remained in the camp, taking care of the kids, talking to other women, and gathering.

So women like to talk. Even though you probably don't need science to back that up, some studies show that women use twice as many words as men do on a daily basis. Of course there are studies to the contrary as well, but, come on, women talk more than men.

That means that women like men that talk! At least at the beginning.

We mentioned previously that women find the following traits attractive: leadership abilities, the ability to empathize and take care of the offspring, and confidence, i.e. the ability of a man to "own his space." A man that doesn't talk very much, or very well, can't really do any of these things can he? A man that can, however, demonstrates his value to women as a potential mate, mainly because he can show off his intelligence, his character, as well as his ability to be an Alpha Male. Alphas have to be good communicators.

So if you are quiet and reserved, it is time to change that, or spend forever not only physically alone, but alone in your head as well. Scientific studies show extroverts, outgoing people who get their energy from others, are on average, happier than introverts, who get their energy from within. Similar studies say that it is possible to convert yourself, or at least move yourself, toward a more extroverted personality. All three authors of this book are extroverted, and our lives are pretty great; we get free stuff all the time from people we just met (because they like us), we influence situations that we find ourselves in, and we are never alone, unless we want to be. It is good to be an extrovert!

That means you need to learn to talk. Talk, talk, talk, talk. If you are shy and introverted, this is one of the most important things you need to change. Talk to strangers, talk to friends! Don't just sit there. Even if all you do is *repeat* the last thing said (as a way of communicating that you "got it") then do that. Watch talk shows, and see how the host talks to the guests. Go to networking events, ask questions, and give longer answers than necessary. If you do this in an intentional way, you will find that people want to talk to you! Many of our clients come to us quiet and introverted, and leave more talkative and outgoing (and happier).

Women love a talkative man, especially if he is interesting and displays excellence. Talking shows that you can lead a conversation, and is a mark of excellence, which is very attractive. So you have to learn to talk.

Routines

Routines are memorized bits of conversation, a kind of "bit," or a "script" that you always have handy in the back of your mind that you can pull out anytime. Now, we are not advocating that all of your conversation becomes "scripted," which is impossible anyway since conversation has interaction, but learning routines can help in a variety of ways.

Getting over approach anxiety is not difficult. You can immunize yourself from, and even embrace, rejection as we have taught you. After a very short time, our clients are able to approach girls with ease. However, after that initial approach most clients find that they run out of stuff to say, usually because they are nervous or they just don't have anything to say. Their body language becomes awkward too (because the brain is signaling "DANGER!" and they clam up even more), and then the girl just stares at them, and they usually have to eject.

Routines help to fix that. If you have some memorized bits of conversation, i.e. you have a little script that you follow, you don't have to think of anything to say, because you already have it. Routines are designed to free you up so you can direct your attention to other things like her body language, or yours. Watch somebody's body language who doesn't know what to say. They clearly look like they don't have anything to say! It looks awkward to say the least.

I want you to think about stand-up comedians again. When they are in front of a crowd, they look completely calm, relaxed, focused, funny, and in control. They engage the crowd like they are talking an old friend. I have done some stand-up in my time (and likewise I use humor in my presentations and motivational speaking) and I can tell you that everything I say, and everything a stand-up comedian says, is *always* scripted. Now that doesn't mean I say the same thing, word-for-word, every time I talk to people, but I generally use the same basic patterns. I know that I am going to say A then B then C. I have the punch lines scripted, I know when people are going to laugh, and I can use the same "material" whether I am in front of 1500 people or one person.

When I do this, I am not being duplicitous. Rather I am using what I know works to create rapport (we will cover this later) between me and my audience, regardless of size. It is possible to build rapport while speaking and presenting, just as it is in conversation, and it is useful to view routines in this light.

Routines are conversation starters, and conversation savers. What I mean is that you need to use routines to get an interaction going, and to give you confidence when you know what you are going to say. It helps you direct and lead the conversation, which is a sign of excellence and attractiveness. The other side of routines is that if a conversation goes stale, then you jump into a routine, which can restart the conversation. You should not rely entirely on routines in a conversation, but normal conversation should flow out of, and back to, your routines naturally.

Sometimes you need two or three routines to get a conversation going, sort of like pulling the starter on a lawn mower. Hopefully, after that, the thing runs on its own, and occasionally you need to pull that starter again if the mower runs out of gas or stalls. Conversations are like mowers!

The reason why stand-up comedians look so funny and natural is that they have practiced their routines 10,000 times, either alone or in an audience. They also are flexible enough to adapt their routines (sometimes on the spot) based on audience and audience response. Look at a guy like Dane Cook. I personally can't stand that guy, and if you have ever seen him twice, you know the guy only has so much material. He tells the same joke, over and over, every time he performs, but his confident delivery is pretty much what provides the humor in his jokes, since, well, a lot of what he says simply isn't funny. Google him, and watch him tell the same joke, the same way, every time he performs. You need to practice your routines in front of a mirror, and with other people, and take a lesson from Dane, and don't use the same material over and over and over again. Always come up with new stuff!

One way to develop new routines is to allow them to naturally emerge in conversation. We find that once we are in great conversational flow, it is easy to deviate from our routines and "ad lib." Typically we will start a conversation with a routine, and then see where it leads. This often leads to new and funny material emerging that later becomes routines (sometimes we are even surprised at what comes out of our mouths!). We now have more original routines than we know what to do with because every conversation is a chance to build new routines. The key is to be flexible and go with the flow.

I love practicing routines on waitresses. Waitresses are perfect because you don't have to deal with approach anxiety. They *have* to talk to you! Use this as an opportunity to practice your routines. Use a different one each time they come to your table. The other nice thing is that they have to be nice to you, since you are going to tip them in the end. If you can make a waitress' day by being a good person, funny, or interesting, she will love you for it. Believe me, most of her customers are probably low-tipping jerks.

I have a routine with waitresses called the "fake relationship." It is really best for waitresses, but gives you an idea about how routines should go.

1. The waitress comes to the table to introduce herself and take our order
2. I say "Oh my gosh, it's you!" pretending to know her
3. Insert a routine, or bit, that you want to practice
4. When she comes back to the table, have a pretend argument like "I thought we were your only table, and here I see you laughing and joking with *that* table there!" Make sure you say it in a joking tone with half a smile on your face.
5. When she comes back, apologize for getting mad, and say "I hope we can move on in our relationship; it wasn't nice of me to yell... I just get so jealous!"

When you use it, it doesn't have to be the same exact, word-for-word, routine. In fact, it shouldn't be, because your "style" won't be the same as mine. However, the "fake fight/relationship" has been a successful way for me to test out routines. You just insert a new routine in step three when you want to try out new material.

One sample routine you could insert at step three would be something like this: "I just wanted you to know that since you didn't give me a free meal last time, Ed said you could give it to me this time, and I won't refuse it." You must say this with confidence and with a slight smile. Invariably she will ask "who's Ed?" You can then assert that it is Ed, the assistant manager, even though you (and she) know that there really is no Ed. Sometimes I glance at the manager's name tag and mention him by name, which makes them gasp in amazement. Most of the time waitresses laugh and act slightly confused when I do this, which is a good thing. Make them wonder about you. Clearly since you are engaging them (something 95% of guys won't do) and acting confidently (again, 95% of guys act shy), they will likely wonder about you *positively*, i.e. think you are a cool and attractive dude.

I am not going to spend much time giving you routines in this book. We will share our unique routines from time-to-time, and may even put them in book form at some point. Be sure to sign up for our newsletter, fan us on Facebook, and follow us on Twitter, to keep updated. You can also Google "conversational routines," and you will find thousands of them. Learn routines and practice them, and most importantly, choose routines that fit your personality, and something that can easily lead to genuine conversation.

Some of my conversational routines are jokes (canned jokes, or ones that I have come up with), some are funny stories, some are topics that I am excellent at talking about (women love that body language stuff we talked about earlier), and some are stories that speak, indirectly, about my excellence. When the time is right, I just pull out the right story/joke/material. I don't really rely on many of the routines that are out there, simply because I come up with my own routines, and since they are mine, I am more comfortable with them. My business partners and I share routines and build off of each other's material. While original routines are ideal, because they will always be fresh to a girl (nothing is worse than when a woman hears the same pick-up line 50 times), a "canned" routine from the internet, executed with confidence, will often work to spark conversation.

Let me elaborate on what I said about being excellent. This is very important: there are routines you need to come up with that *indirectly* talk about your excellence. For instance, I have mentioned a few indirect ones in this book already that show my value. I have talked about being in Rome as a tour guide. I would never walk up to someone and say directly that I studied in Rome, therefore I am special. It looks desperate. The same is true with men that flaunt their money. Plenty of girls have told me that men have walked up to them just to tell them how rich they were. Those girls told me how happy they were to walk away from those dudes.

Demonstrations of your excellence and value need to be woven into your conversation. Again, when I told the story of Rome and the Russian girl, it was a pertinent part of what I was saying, but the value and excellence come in two ways. One, that I can meet and talk to pretty girls, and two, that I have spent time in foreign countries. You want to talk about things that make you seem awesome, but it needs to be said indirectly. If you can weave your excellence and value into the conversation, she will find that attractive. A good way to do that is: "Hey that reminds me of that time I was in Rome when I..." You are mentioning your time abroad as a part of the larger context of the story, and she will pick up on that and file it away in the "valuable" part of her brain. That is a good way a routine can turn into a normal conversation, because I promise you, she will ask about Rome once you give her a chance to speak.

Now, let me share a brief word about "openers" or opening routines. These are the first things you say to someone when you are first meeting them. Some of the routines you will find on the internet are too long and drawn out to be good openers. Openers should but short, sweet, and to the point. They should be a little shocking too, in order to throw them off guard. One of my favorites is, "are you a vegetarian?" Usually they freeze (limbic system kicking in), ponder, and then answer yes or no, to which I have a response prepared. If they are, say, "Oh no! Weirdo!" And if not, I say, "That's good, because those people are weird!" Then go into a longer routine. I should note that whenever you talk to women like this, it must be done playfully, because you do not want to make them defensive.

Remember, they are expecting you to lead the conversation when you first meet them, in order to see if you are dominant, confident, a leader, etc. Of course, when you get into a relationship with them, that probably flips, and they end up being the more talkative ones. How to be in a relationship will be the topic of another Joe Alpha Factor book. There are a lot more things to talk about regarding routines, and whole books of routines are out there, but the most important thing is that you go armed into *any* conversation, be it with a woman, boss, interviewer, etc., with an arsenal of well memorized scripts that make you look intelligent and confident, which can start or save a conversation. I have routines for every aspect of my life, whether I am talking to women, CEOs of companies, academics, baristas, servers, religious people, etc., and thus I am never ever left without something to say!

Chapter Eighteen: Demonstrate Value: If you Can't Be Funny, Be Interesting

So at this point of the game, you should be able to walk confidently into a room, own your space, approach people, especially women, with poise and confidence, have some bits of conversation in routines, make some physical contact, and recognize when she is attracted to you. Hopefully, you are also learning how to transition into normal conversation, communicating based on the spontaneity of the conversation, and not reliant entirely on routines. As I have mentioned earlier in this book, you should dissect each one of those moments in the initial part of a conversation, and practice each one individually. Have a night where all you are doing is approaching, followed by a night where you are working on one routine. Practice, practice, practice! Remember when you first learned how to shoot a basketball or throw a football? What was initially awkward become natural after practicing. This is how you want to approach meeting people.

These are all technical aspects of how to approach people in general, and women specifically. The dynamic really doesn't change depending on whom you are approaching, because we are all wired pretty much the same. These initial steps are of the highest importance, because the first impression you make is the impression you will have to live with, so you might as well make that impression as a confident Alpha Male. There will be times in which you will slip and lose some confidence in your conversation, where it will run out of steam, where she will get a call, when her friends will try to break her away, or whatever. When that happens, you are going to need that first impression as a confident Alpha Male to push you past those weaker moments.

Think of stand-up comedians again. They use some of their best material right out of the chute (to give you a strong first impression, which you will carry with you through their show), then in the middle they use weaker material (using the momentum of the first impression to get them through), and finally they end on some of their best material again, so that you will confirm your first impression of them, and want to buy their products or see them again when they are in town. You need to do the same thing.

First impressions are of utmost importance, because when we first encounter anything, a new restaurant, city, person, or whatever, that first impression makes the brain wire in a stimulus-response circuit. What I mean to say is that the brain will automatically wire when it encounters something new based on the response you get the first time. That wiring is hard to break and will frame how that person experiences that new stimulus in the future. The more that wiring is confirmed, or used, the more solid that wiring becomes. So you want people to "wire positively" to you the first time they meet you. It has been said that people make instantaneous impressions of people the first time they meet them, in the first four or five seconds. That is why your posture and body language, even before you meet them, is of extreme importance, as they are already sizing you up.

Once you make that first approach, and get that great first impression of being detached, excellent, and confident, you need to reinforce that good first impression by what you say and do, in order to "hard wire" their brains to respond positively when you interact with them. This is not only important in the initial meeting, but subsequent meetings as well.

We had a client in The Joe Alpha Factor who was great at approaches. He could approach anybody, anytime, anywhere. He was a quiet guy when we met him, and still is to some extent, but his problem wasn't the approach. It was the follow up. He could not have a conversation naturally with the people he had just met. He would execute two or three of our routines, then clam up, just standing there awkwardly for a few seconds before turning tail and running. Eventually, we got him to break that habit and learn the art of conversation.

Throughout this book we have mentioned being excellent and showing high value. If you are going to attract women, you *have* to do both. Women are not attracted to low value men, or men that cannot demonstrate detachment and excellence. There are a couple of ways to do this without coming off like you are *trying* to show value and excellence, as I mentioned in the last chapter. You want this to look natural.

First and foremost, you need to believe that you are both excellent and valuable. If you don't believe it, neither will they. As we mentioned earlier, go and be excellent at whatever you are excellent at, on the day you are going to go out and meet women. Then, carry that feeling of excellence with you wherever you go.

Humor

A great way to show excellence is humor. Not everyone is funny. Some people are naturally funny, and others have to learn it. It is something you can learn with some time. Humor is of the highest importance because it shows women that you are intelligent. Back when we all lived in the forest and had to survive there, intelligent males survived the best, because they were quicker to adapt. Strength and speed give out a lot more quickly than intelligence, and, while it is safe to say that the strong and fast have some early advantage (for example the captain of the football team in High School), intelligent males have the longer term advantage. The strong and quick guy might try to take on a bear, while the intelligent male would try to outwit it. Guess which survived?

For example, compare the most excellent in two fields, sports and computers. LeBron James makes about $40 million a year. Bill Gates is worth *billions*. In the long term, the smarter guys, even in our culture, have the best earnings, and therefore survival power. Even in sports the most successful athletes are the ones that made intelligent business decisions. Ten years after high school, the captain of the football team might be a fry-cook, while the smart guy is president of a company and making millions.

For a male to be attractive, he has to have the one-two punch of intelligence and social graces, which culminate as humor. I remember seeing an interview with supermodel Christie Brinkley back in the 1980s when she was at her best looking. She was asked to identify the sexiest man in the world. Without any hesitation she identified comedian John Candy. John Candy was 6'4" tall with 400+ pounds of mostly fat. He was by no means the sleek and fast dude women are supposed to be attracted to. She said that a sense of humor is the sexiest trait a man can have. If Christie Brinkley isn't proof enough, I should point out that John Candy made Playgirl Magazine's list of most desirable men in 1985.

I have known generally average looking guys physically outclassed by the weight lifters and body builders who probably could not get away with the tight t-shirts that body builders and tough guys wear. However, I can guarantee you that when it comes to women, I have seen average looking guys outclass those physically dominant types of guys almost every single time. I have seen them whisk their women away right in front of them on numerous occasions, and the weapon that guys like that have to thank for that is their sense of humor.

Sometimes they use routines, like I have mentioned previously. Sometimes they are spontaneously funny, which is a skill that I had to *learn* over the years. Sometimes it is a mix of the two, but whether it is naturally off-the-cuff, or a routine, it always looks natural when the real Alpha Males do it. The only time it is clearly "unnatural" is if they am telling a straight joke. Don't rely on those, though. Jokes are for guys that aren't really funny (this applies to social media status updates as well - don't be the guy whose statuses are dumb recycled online jokes!).

It is true that some people are born with the ability to be funny, but it is possible to develop it too. How do you become funny? I myself had to develop a sense of humor. I simply watched funny people being funny. I studied them, got a sense of their timing, and learned what worked for them and what didn't. The funny people I modeled had to work on being funny too, since nobody comes out of the womb being the funniest man alive. So I modeled them in every way possible. I stood like they did. I said the things they said. I learned their patterns and routines, and eventually it became a part of me, modified, of course, based on my personality. I remember in high school trying all sorts of things that weren't funny. I got a lot of strange looks, but, through trial and error, I developed my style of humor. As quick material, I just stole lines from the Simpsons or funny movies, so I could focus on my timing. After a while, I started developing my own material, and finally I was able to be funny off the cuff. As I mentioned previously, I love coming up with new spontaneous material, and, if it works, I remember it and turn it into a new routine.

Humor is so attractive because it really is a combination of many attractive traits. Humor is intelligence, social grace, excellence, and status all in one. Everyone loves people with a sense of humor, and will bend over backwards to please them. Having a sense of humor is very helpful when making a first impression. However, just being funny isn't enough, and you have to transition to other levels of excellence, which we will cover in a few paragraphs.

Teasing

When I was in 4th grade I was head-over-heels for a girl named Lacy. Lacy was blond and cute, and many years later she is still as cute as ever. I spent all day making fun of her in class. I had mean names for her. I pulled her hair, and I got others to make fun of her.... and she *loved* it.

Girls loved to be teased- it is the best kind of flirting that there is. Remember, the funniest jokes are the ones that are a little true, so making fun of her or teasing her is a great way to get a girl to like you. It has to be done in a nice tone, and with a smile on your face, to let her know you are joking around. You don't actually want to insult her directly, although I have said some pretty nasty things to a girl and gotten her to follow me home.

I generally keep it on the teasing level, playful and fun. However, I can give you an example of a more insulting version of this too. Either way, whether you tease in a playful or more insulting way, it has to be done confidently, with relaxed body language, or you look like a weirdo. One thing you must keep in mind when you "neg" a girl is that you are flirting with her. Always keep this in mind.

We often take clients to festivals as part of their training (it is a great place to meet a lot of people). One of our clients, a 22 year old guy, and I wanted to experiment with this borderline insult concept. So, I told him to approach a slender girl and say "you are pretty cute for a big girl." The girl was not big at all, and looked like she never was (you could tell). He did what he was told, confidently, with a big smile on his face. He said his comment, waited for the "freeze" response to kick in, and turned and walked away. She ended up chasing him, grabbing him, getting (fake) mad at him, and by the end, she gave him her phone number and insisted that he call her. Her friends thought it was funny too. You will get blowback from this type of "neg," but it may work out for you in the end, especially if you are confident, and even a little cocky about it.

Let me tell you another story about the power of teasing. I knew a cute girl in high school that everybody else pretty much hated. She was cute, but mean and generally hostile toward others. Most guys (beta males) responded to her sarcasm either by trying to kiss up to her, or getting frustrated and angrily yelling at her. However, not me. I responded to her by teasing her, i.e. playfully teasing her. The result? She became totally cool and was nice to me.

In fact, I even dated her sister for a while. As I mentioned, the effectiveness of teasing seems counter-intuitive, i.e. everything we have been told by teachers and parents says it doesn't work. But I promise you, if it is done confidently, flirtatiously, and in a way that is *not creepy,* it will work!

Why Teasing Works

There are a million reasons why this works, and a million reasons why it seems counter intuitive. You probably learned from your mom, dad, and teachers, either directly or indirectly, that to impress women, you must be "nice" to them. Basically, you are supposed to kiss butt, and if you do that enough, they will like you enough to be your girlfriend or wife. That is how Beta Males operate. They essentially "bribe" women into being interested in them. This is a type of manipulation (as all communication is). The Beta is definitely manipulating each time he tries to "bribe" a girl into liking him with compliments, gifts, or favors. In the end, because bribery shows a person isn't confident or excellent, it backfires, and she puts him in the "friend zone," saying something like "you're a nice guy," or "you remind me of my brother."

As we have said time and time again, women don't want nice and passive guys. They want assertive, confident, capable and excellent men. Hell, that doesn't just apply to women. If I am an employer looking to hire, I don't want some butt kisser that is telling me what he thinks I want to hear. I want someone with the initiative and confidence to get the job done right. The material we are presenting teaching in this book applies to every situation in your life. If you are kissing butt, or bribing someone, that does not exemplify any of those positive qualities I just listed. If you are excellent, then why do you have to bribe anyone into liking you? Your value will speak for itself.

So, Alpha Males naturally tease females. Notice I said *females*. Have you ever noticed that dads interact with their daughters by slightly teasing them? Teasing females comes naturally to males. It is probably built into our wiring. In fact, this is one reason why fathers are so important in the lives of children. Dads actually immunize their daughters against jerks by teasing them slightly as children.

So why do Alphas naturally tease? You are humorous (read: intelligent), detached, and assertive, and, by teasing a girl, you are letting her know from the start that you are detached enough not to care if she goes away. Usually that means she won't go away at all. The prettier a girl is, the more you have to tease her, because the prettier she is, the more her butt is usually kissed by the millions (billions?) of Beta Males roaming the earth.

Another reason teasing works is the same reason the "breaking rapport" tactic works. It is sort of a "mini-flight," a way of "being gone," as we talked about in the Tao of Steve. It gives the impression of social exclusion. Remember, our brains react *very* negatively to social exclusion. The more we push people away, the more they tend to pursue us. So in a sense, by teasing them, you are making them chase you by pushing them away with your comments. It actually shuts down their natural defenses, and makes them want to be part of your "tribe."

A final reason teasing works is related to value. As I mentioned, people want to see value in you, and I suspect you want people to see value in you as well. We all like to feel valuable. We want to know we are worth something, and most people will do anything to do get that acknowledgment.

Women are insecure. All of them. They are, as we have discussed in this book, passive in nature. They defend their insecurities with a finely sharpened sword. They are also used to being chased for their positive traits, and hate being criticized for their negatives. When you tease, you are pushing those insecurity buttons, and all of a sudden their "apparent" value has dropped, so they will try to prove their value to you, because they really want to feel valuable themselves! When you push those insecurity buttons in a way that is flirtatious and non-threatening, all of a sudden people, especially women, will do anything to prove you wrong, and prove themselves valuable. All of a sudden, they will be chasing you!

Let me tell you about a client we had that was out getting "shot down," to get him over his approach anxiety. It was the end of the night, and he was tired of approaching groups of girls, and wanted to have a drink (we make everyone work sober in our program, because "liquid courage" is not real courage). I told him that he had to approach one more group before he could start drinking. I picked the absolute most beautiful group in the place. He was hesitant, even though he had just experienced a lot of success that night (which, incidentally, happens on the shoot down night). So he reluctantly approached those pretty girls, and to his surprise, they wouldn't let him go! Now, he wasn't to the point of teasing yet, but why is it that they wouldn't let him leave?

The answer is simple. The prettier the girl, the more insecure everyone is. Men don't approach them (out of fear), and so the pretty girls begin to feel self-conscious about themselves and will take anyone who approaches them! So, when it comes to really pretty girls, remember that they are the most insecure of all! However, remember that they require more teasing, since the guys that do talk to them usually kiss their asses so bad they are chapped

Less attractive girls deal with their insecurities in another way: they usually get mean. It is funny how that works. You might think that approaching a girl who is a 7 or 8 is easier than approaching the 9 or 10. I have found the opposite. The less attractive a girl is, the meaner she tends to be. That is because she knows that she isn't as pretty, so all of her defenses are up to protect her insecurities, which are constantly being called out, not only by herself internally, but by everyone who sees her. She is not complimented like the 9 or

10, which at least helps the 9 or 10 not to feel as bad. The less attractive girl will actually try to stop you from talking to her more attractive friend because of all the mixed up stuff going on in their head. So, don't somehow think that approaching a 7 or 8 will be easier than approaching the prettiest girl in the room.

However, always remember our rule: treat everyone the same. Tease them all, 6 and 10 alike, and they will love you. Just make sure your teasing doesn't cross the line to hurt their feelings. However, if you do cross line, don't start with the comforting Beta Male behavior just to win her back. Apologize if necessary, but don't start kissing her butt to make her feel better. Teasing does not mean becoming a Gamma male jerk, although that pretty much works too. Weird huh?

On that note, by the way, you probably are aware how successful Gamma Males (the jerks) are with women. Pretty much every "nice guy" has been rejected because a woman was dating a jerk loser. Gammas are often successful *because* they treat women badly. We are not recommending you treat women badly, but it shows that even taking teasing to extremes actually attracts a decent number of women.

There are many evolutionary dynamics, brain wiring, etc., that we could cover to explain why teasing is attractive, but that is beyond the scope of the book. The way you learn to tease is by first teasing your guy friends. By sitting around making fun of each other you will learn to do it when you meet women. See, treat everyone the same, even your buddies. Always tease graciously, with a smile on your face (an Alpha Smile, not a Beta one).

Remember, girls like being teased if you make it funny for them. The way you know if you are doing it right is that they will "smack" you in a playful way (kino). They will also uncontrollably laugh, or gasp with their mouths wide like an "O," pretending they are shocked and appalled! That is the reaction you want! When they pretend to be upset, you have succeeded. Note that I said "pretend," because their body language clearly indicates they are enjoying it. Girls *love* to be teased by Alpha Males.

If You Can't Be Funny, Be Interesting

Some guys just aren't funny. Some guys will never be funny. Some people try to be funny and aren't. Being funny is an art form that can be learned, somewhat, but there is nothing worse than someone *trying* to be funny (and probably looking creepy too!), who isn't. Of course, nobody likes anyone who has to try too hard at anything. That, again, is our definition of a Beta Male. Excellence is natural and comes from practice.

So, learn how to be funny. As I mentioned above, model funny people, and pay attention to how they talk and move, and their timing. Steal material from them, and from movies and TV shows until you can come up with your own unique type of humor. Invent routines or "bits" that are funny pieces of conversation that you can use with different people. Practice being funny with your friends before you try it on women. Stand-up comic Gabriel Iglesias said an interview that he wrote his material by getting together once a week with his buddies with the intent of just being funny with each other, i.e. to tease and jab each other verbally. Today he is a very successful comedian.

Whenever I meet people in any situation, I usually lead with my sense of humor (I have a lot of great funny material that I have developed, and yes, I occasionally use bits I from TV or movies if appropriate.

But if you can't be funny, be interesting. Girls like to talk about relationship stuff a lot, but if you can work your excellence at something into the conversation you will usually be successful, because doing so is interesting and socially acceptable. Remember to keep the topics *interesting for them too*! So DON'T talk about your latest World of Warcraft campaign, but DO talk about your friend's problem with the girl that is stalking him online! It is important to be able to be captivating, either by humor or being genuinely interesting. Don't forget, women *love* giving advice. So posing an opinion question (like "My friend wants to get engaged, but doesn't know if he still needs to ask her dad or not.") to get a conversation started is a great way to begin a normal conversation, and for you to disarm them.

At this point, you should re-read this book's section on body language, because it is great material. Sometimes I just talk to girls about body language, and have fun pointing out things that are happening in the room with other people. It makes you look very high value and excellent, and the body language stuff is always interesting to them, since it is essentially a relationship matter. Also, it puts you on "the same side," when you are talking about people in the room.

Remember, if you can't be funny, be interesting, and have lots of good material to talk about. I treat everyone the same, and realize that everyone is practice.

Chapter Nineteen: Building Rapport and Making Connections

Whether that relationship lasts five minutes or thirty years, we want you to always leave women, and people in general, better off than you found them. Trust me, if you do that, people will flock around you, men and women alike, and you will be the creator of your own reality with tons of people to support you.

That is where The Joe Alpha Factor really shines. While most of this book is how to meet and be attractive to women, the essence of our program is really based on how to establish good, mutually beneficial relationships with all people. This book is really about creating a first impression, so that you come off as a confident and assertive Alpha Male, who is a leader of men and attractive to women, someone who owns his space, and helps others as he helps himself.

That being said, this chapter is going to explain how to make a connection with others, at least initially, so that you can continue the relationship at another time. Relationships, in general, are very complex things, and we certainly aren't going to go into the deep ins-and-outs of long term relationships here. We will save that for another book. However all long term relationships start with a meeting and a good first impression. You have to meet them, demonstrate excellence and value, and create a connection that will make others want to deepen your relationship with them.

Rapport: Establishing a Deeper Connection

Most of this book thus far has been geared toward giving you strategies to reach two well-formed outcomes. The first outcome has been to develop your inner "game" and focus. We have taught you how to reframe the way that you think about yourself and your social interactions with groups and individuals. This reframe allows you to easily overcome defense and survival mechanisms that evolution has placed in your brain - and the brains of the women you want to talk to. In other words, improving your mental game gives you a social edge, and the ability to approach people without setting off their alarms, or, for that matter, your alarms related to approach anxiety.

The second outcome is to enter people's lives so they want you to stay in their lives, and, in turn, to attract even more people into your life. We have provided you the strategies to get to this point.

Once you have reached these outcomes (and it takes time; keep practicing the techniques we have given you) it is important to know how to establish a connection with people. We call this "building rapport." Our goal is to help you establish that connection with others that you deeply desire, a connection of body, mind, and soul.

One of our clients, whom I mentioned above, was great at approaches, but couldn't form connections with people. He could approach all day long, get people to talk to him, and then all of a sudden he would freeze, turn, and leave. It was a great day when we saw him start to change and talk to people for more than five minutes at a time, and even better when he got his first girlfriend.

As we have covered previously, humans are essentially social. Being social is a huge part of what makes us a human, namely that we can enter into, and maintain, relationships with other humans. Have you ever met someone that couldn't? They are "weird." Our brains are wired to be social from the beginning, and the first connection we have is with our own mothers. Even in the womb a baby establishes a relationship and builds rapport.

Mirror Neurons and Tribalism

Earlier, we talked about a person being considered a "foe," when we initially meet them, or they meet us. We have frequently addressed how to overcome that natural tendency so that you can present yourself as a "friend," or at the very least, not a threat.

Now that you are there, it is time to deepen the relationship with the person you have met. They think you are safe enough to talk to. They see some value and excellence in you. You are funny, or at least interesting. It is time to ramp that up.

In the brains of many animals, including mammals, birds, fish, and other creatures, there is a network of neurons called "mirror neurons." A great book on the subject is The Tell-Tale Brain: A

<u>Neuroscientist's Quest for What Makes Us Human</u>, by V.S. Ramachandran.

Mirror neurons have all sorts of great functions, most of which we won't cover here. But for our purposes, they tell us one thing: this person *is*, or this person *is not*, like me. This is vitally important to building rapport.

Let's revisit a concept that we briefly mentioned before: tribalism. Tribalism is alive and well among humans. When we were in the forest, the jungle, and the desert, we relied on each other for survival. To be excluded from a tribe meant that you had to go it alone, therefore, essentially it meant death. Tribes helped us forage, collect, hunt, and raise children - in essence to survive. We are fundamentally wired for survival and humans learned pretty early on that survival is easier through cooperation.

That tribal mentality is built into the very core of who we are. Imagine what might have happened 25,000 years ago, when two tribes met. All of a sudden, the limited resources of one tribe were in danger of being used by the other tribe. If we are wired for survival, which we are, that means that if our resources are cut in two, we may not survive, so something had to be done. When two "tribes" meet, one of three things will happen: One will annihilate the other, they will annihilate each other, or they will merge into a bigger tribe.

This tribal mentality is one of the reasons why new people, that is, people that are not in our current tribe, are regarded as foes. Every new "tribe" we meet is a threat to our resources, our relationships, and our livelihood. This is why it is our "default" setting is to assume "foe" before "friend."

Tribalism, while it has changed forms in modern culture, is still pretty much the same today. The Middle East is a perfect example, where countries like Iraq are still essentially conglomerations of smaller tribes. In this sense, nothing has changed. But in our modern culture, tribalism expresses itself in divisions of race/ethnicity (white, black, Hispanic etc.), politics (Democrat/Republican), class (wealthy/poor), religion (Catholic, Protestant, Jew, Muslim, etc.), criminal association (gangs, crime syndicates), and even in the sports teams we support! Sports teams are easy to identify because members proudly wear their "tribal" colors.

If you don't think that modern "tribes" won't try to annihilate each other, just watch a soccer game in South America, where riots are commonplace when one's team loses. Watch a Protestant and a Catholic have a debate, and you'll see tribalism in action. In Ireland, those two groups of Christians killed each other for decades.

Essentially, what we have taught you here in the preceding chapters of this book is how to enter into a new tribe: how to present yourself in a way that doesn't set off any mental danger alarms, to indicate that you won't assault them or steal their "resources." Approach a group with both men and women, and see how the men react to you. We will teach you how to overcome this in an upcoming chapter.

One of the ways that we overcome the problem of tribalism, no matter what tribe you are in (and you are probably in several) is found in the mirror neurons. When the mirror neurons see someone that is like them, they register "friend." When they detect tribal differences, such as race, class, etc., they automatically register "foe." We are nice to our friends, we don't try to kill them, and we share our resources with them, and they with us. We don't treat our foes the same way, do we?

So the key to really deepening rapport, that connection with people, is to be found in our brain's mirror neurons.

Let me give you an example before we go on. When I lived in Italy in the early 2000s, it was clear that I was different. I am 6'3". I have fair skin, blue eyes, and reddish blond hair. It is clear that I was not like most Italians, who are shorter, olive skinned, and have dark hair (some have blue eyes). It was clear that I was not one of the "tribe," and often I was treated with trepidation, an effect that was more stark before I learned the language. I even dressed differently than they did.

When I met Americans in Italy, the story was different. You can hear Americans from a mile away. We are loud, and we wear baggy clothes and white tennis shoes. We are often ethnically diverse (one of the first "tribes" to do this with some success, that is, the "American Tribe"), and the most important thing is how we speak English. When I was in Italy or Mexico (I lived there for a while too, and I fit in even less!), and would hear English, that would be enough to let me be instant friends with other Americans. I was always instant friends with Americans (and not even English tourists) because when I spoke American English, the mirror neurons in the brains of the other Americans registered "friend," because they told the brain: "This guy is *like* me, so he is my friend and part of the same 'tribe.'" People that I would have *never* talked to in the U.S., where our "tribal" differences would be more apparent, were my best friends in foreign countries.

Once I learned Italian, and started to set off the mirror neurons of my Italian acquaintances, the same thing happened: they accepted me into their "tribe." That is why when I go to a foreign country, by the way, I learn at least a snippet of the language, like "thank you," or "good morning." You wouldn't believe how far that gets you with people of another "tribe."

So when it comes to creating that sense of "comfort," "rapport," and connection, if you can fire off their mirror neurons, that sense of connection will be instantaneous. Imagine creating instantaneous connections with people. It is possible, and even easier than you think.

When I was in Italy, I learned that in order to establish a deeper connection with Americans I met, I would try to find even more "in common," with them. If they said they were from Oklahoma, I would say: "My uncle teaches at Oklahoma State University!" which he does. If they said Utah, I would say "Oh I have friends in Utah." I wouldn't necessarily make things up, but what I was intuitively doing (I say "intuitively" because I hadn't read about mirror neurons) was firing off their mirror neurons, even if the connection was tenuous at best! It worked like a charm, and still does when I meet anyone. I find commonalities, even if they are minor, which puts us in the same "tribe."

Firing Off Their Mirror Neurons and Becoming Part of the Tribe

There are several easy ways to fire off someone's mirror neurons. We do it to each other all the time. A university study tested students by dressing up someone who resembled them physically in the same way that the test subject was dressed. In other words, they made someone up to look just like the subjects. Almost 100% of the time, when that student walked into the lecture hall and saw a person that resembled them, they sat beside, immediately in front of, or in back of the person, or at the very least near their doppelganger, within one or two rows. The same effect was not observed when the test subject entered a room with someone of a different ethnicity. The test subjects tended to sit, on average, farther away (no closer than 3 or 4 rows) from the person that was ethnically different from themselves and the rest of the class.

These kids were not bigots or racists, but their mirror neurons told the rest of the brain that this person was not in their "tribe." So the conclusion is simple: be like the person you are trying to talk to. This goes beyond what I wrote about my experience in Europe, where I simply found things in common like Oklahoma or Utah, but if you really want to make a good connection with someone, it can, and almost has, to go deeper.

There is a concept in many sales and self-help books called "mirroring" or "pacing." They are essentially two different words for the same concept, although each contains a subtle difference. Pacing and mirroring is where you match the vocabulary, the body language, and even involuntary activities like blinking and breathing, in order to build rapport and fire off their mirror neurons.

Pacing

Pacing refers more to mimicking people's vocabulary, rate of speech, and even their basic beliefs, in other words agreeing with them, when you can. A clear example is when I was speaking in the South over the summer. I am from the North, and specifically the

Midwest, and I was invited to speak at a conference in Jackson, Mississippi. In the South, they speak more slowly, have an accent (different depending on which part of the South you go!), and use a somewhat different vocabulary. When I started to speak to anyone in the South, I saw the "freeze" response. It was clear that I was not of the "Southern Tribe."

We northerners do the same thing. We judge southerners on how they speak. Since they speak more slowly, we think they are not as smart, which is not the case. They sometimes dress differently and have different values. So I imagine we northerners sound like we are talking 1000 miles per hour.

While in the South, I remembered everything I am writing about here, and I began to slow down my speech, and repeat some of their different vocabulary. I didn't do it overtly, but every so often, I worked in one of "their" words. Things started to go a lot more smoothly after that.

So, if you meet a girl and she talks really fast, pace her, and speed up your pace. Further, if she is using a particular word a lot, let's say "awesome," then work the word "awesome" into the conversation. You want it to look like a natural part of your speech, not something you are trying to throw in just to sound like her.

Finally, you can pace concepts. The words "I agree" are very powerful words. If she says something you can agree with, say "I agree that (whatever she just said)." Nod your head as well, to pace her with your body language. Just repeat back to her the last part of her sentence with the words "I agree" attached. Again, do this subtly, and not after every sentence she says.

Example:

> Her: I think the Red Hot Chili Peppers are the best band ever!
>
> You: I agree that the Red Hot Chili Peppers are the best band ever!

It doesn't have to be a word-for-word agreement. You are pacing, not mocking. You can say "I agree; the Red Hot Chili Peppers are one of the best bands I have heard." The point is that you are getting into what salesmen call an "agree set" or "yes set," and the more of those you get her into, the more rapport you will build, and the more she will trust you.

If you don't agree with what she says (and you shouldn't agree just to agree like Beta Males do), you can even say "I agree that you said that the Red Hot Chili Peppers are the best band ever." You aren't agreeing with the concept, but with the fact that she said it. It still fires off the mirror neurons. You should make sure that you disagree with her about some things, because it shows you are an independent thinker, which means you are excellent and detached.

<u>Mirroring</u>

Mirroring is a similar concept to pacing, but it involves physical "pacing." It is literally what it sounds like it is. When they move their arm to take a drink, you move your arm, the one that mirrors them (that is, as if they are looking in a mirror), and you take a drink. It doesn't have to be at exactly the same time, but can be thirty seconds later. It has to look natural, because you don't want to look like you are making fun of them or acting creepy.

You don't have to do exactly what she is doing. If she takes a drink with her right hand, you can use a napkin to wipe your mouth with your left hand (if you are facing her, the hand across from her right hand). This has the same effect on the mirror neurons, which tells her brain "this person is like me!" You don't have to mirror every movement either, or it will look like you are imitating her, or poking fun. You don't want that. This should be subtle and natural, or else you will set off the "freeze, flight, or fight," part of her brain.

If you are trying to be super subtle, or even more effective, you can even breathe and blink at the same pace as them. I find this rather unnecessary, and frankly, too much work. But it works effectively, and is a very quick way to build rapport without them knowing it. You want to do this kind of thing when you are listening to her talk. Again, I think it is overkill, and takes too much attention to be effective, especially with all the other stuff you need to do.

Have you ever wondered why people that have been married for fifty years start looking like brother and sister? It happens a lot. This is because for fifty years both spouses have been unconsciously making the same facial gestures, as they have naturally mirrored each other. Their faces eventually begin to grow old alike! When people have rapport, they will naturally mirror each other, so to some, mirroring is more of a sign of rapport than something that causes it, but in my experience, I know that mirroring not only proves rapport, but builds it and deepens it.

Rapport, built this way, is cumulative. That is, if you built rapport with someone the first time you meet them and then use these techniques later, it builds on the previous experiences.

Leading

Once you have effectively paced and mirrored someone, you can actually begin to lead them! That's right! We have referred to Robert Cialdini's book, <u>Influence</u> earlier in this book. In his book, he explains a law of influence called the "Law of Liking." When people like you, they are more likely to do things for you, or to at the very least follow your "lead." A test of this is after you have mirrored them for a bit, do something different, like break rapport (which we referred to as "punishment" in the body language section of this book). If they follow you, and begin to mirror you, or try to reestablish rapport, you have them. If they don't, go back to pacing and mirroring. It doesn't take much to test this, and as before, be subtle. If they like you, they will follow you, and to get them to like you, build rapport using the techniques that we have outlined above.

So a few months ago, we took out some clients to teach them some of the wisdom that is in this book. When we are with clients, they get our full attention, since we are there to make sure they are successful. There was a girl there, whom we later found out was named "Jenna." Jenna fit the bill. She was clearly a crazy party girl, beautiful and the center of attention

She was dancing on a little stage that was in the club, immediately across from another little stage, that was empty. Now generally I don't recommend dancing, as we have talked about above in our discussion of environments to meet women. However, this was not a dance club, so these were two little stages that were probably reserved for professional dancers at one time.

I told one of the clients, who we had taught pacing and leading to, to run over to her, looked up, and say, "I am going to out dance you! Dance off!" She laughed (because she is a pretty girl, and he was about 5'5" and chubby), and he ran over to the opposite stage, and began to mirror her moves as best as he could. He did this for about a minute, then he started doing something else, and she started to mirror HIM! It was great!

After that, he went back to her and confidently said that she had lost! She almost attacked him (in a good way) when he walked past her (ignoring her completely, of course) a few minutes later. She hugged him, kissed him, and he kissed her back, and we left. When we came back later, she did it all again. It was a great night. I am sure she is a man eater, but it is great to get the man eaters to chase you, and you then toss them away like they do to so many poor Beta Males. By the way, while she was in the midst of hugging and kissing him, we were waiting by the door, and the bouncer pointed at our client and said: "That guy is awesome." See guys, everyone is watching! Work the whole room.

He did that without saying much of anything to her. It was all done through pacing and leading

You can practice pacing and leading on anyone. The more you practice, the more effective you will become. It is a quick way to get people to like you, and when people like you, and feel a connection with you, they are more apt to do things for you. They will give you a job, go out on a date, and forgive you when the Beta Male in you comes out (which it will). Go to the mall or a restaurant and just observe rapport among people there. It is easy to see which couples have rapport and which don't; the ones that do will be naturally pacing and mirroring each other.

Chapter Twenty: Closing and Follow Up

This book is about starting relationships: how to enter and work a room, meeting people, proving yourself a "friend," entering into other "tribes," and building initial rapport. Eventually, the first meeting will come to an end, and you will part ways.

While you are building rapport, it is possible several things will happen. If you are in a club, while you are building rapport, you may also be escalating kino (touching), and you may kiss her. It happens, and you can actually do it often if you are good at proving your value and building rapport. If that is what you are looking for, then the techniques in this book will help you get there.

We at The Joe Alpha Factor emphasize building relationships, and teach clients more than just how to pick up women Other books by The Joe Alpha Factor Series will explain with how to be in relationships with people, men and women both, for mutual benefit.

Let's say, though, that you are in this to form genuine mutually giving relationships, where you can be the Alpha Male that women are attracted to, and men want to follow. So you have to find some way to continue the relationship after the initial meeting. In some ways this is as equally difficult as the approach, because this is another situation that your brain, wired for survival, tells you that you might get killed. Getting shot down and getting "killed" are the same thing to the brain.

There is an old concept in sales called "ABC," or "Always Be Closing." I hope that you can see how our techniques can also be applied to other things, like a job interview, or even being a good salesman. The dynamics behind human nature are universal and apply across many types of relationships. While the focus of this book is meeting women, the concepts are helpful in just about any area of your life. An Alpha Male can flexibly apply quality and successful strategies in any situation he faces.

A "close," is the outcome you want to achieve in any given situation. If you are a salesman, a close is completing the sale to a client. A close for someone on a job interview is getting the job. A close for an Alpha Male is the continuation of a relationship, and their integration into your tribe, or your integration into their tribe (as a leader of course!). No matter what your desired outcome, "the close" should be the driving factor behind your activities, and something that is on your mind. ABC means that you should always have the end in mind, and tailor all of your activities toward the achievement of that end.

Whether you are interested in developing an initial interaction into a friendship or romantic relationship is up to you, and both have deep value. Either way, the close is important. We define "closing" as finding a way to continue a relationship past the first meeting.

First, this is a hard and fast rule that you need to remember: *You* are the one that needs to end the encounter. If she ends it, that means you are chasing her. You want her to chase you! So, in any situation, you have to end the interaction. This goes for chatting, texting, meeting, hanging out, etc. There are a variety of reasons for this. To outline a few, this shows that you are detached, and not hyper focused. Detachment and confidence are related as we have covered. It also shows that you can be "gone," which will enact the "Law of Scarcity." When a resource is scarce, it becomes more valuable, even if you are that resource! Finally, it shows confidence, in that you are confident and detached enough to not worry about losing her. So, you end the conversations and interactions. Make her the last to text, to chat, and you be the first to say "I need to get going." You should leave at a *high point* of the conversation, not when it is waning. Always leave them wanting more. Remember our stand-up comedian friends who always end a show with their best material.

Ending an encounter on a high point will be difficult. Your natural desire will be to want to keep the momentum going, because you will be enjoying yourself if you have done your job and built rapport. Tearing yourself away when you really want to stay is a very Alpha thing to do, and it is a very necessary thing to do to show you are in control of a situation. This is even true in romantic relationships that have become physical. Try it, when you get to that point with a girl, while you are kissing her, just, for no reason, stop. It will drive her nuts, in a good way!

So, you are at the high point of a conversation, building great rapport, and you decide it is time to go. All you need to say is, "I need to go." Have something in mind, and don't just stand on the other side of the bar where they can see you. Have another group to talk to, visit with your friends, or just leave. As an Alpha Male, you are a busy and valuable man, and you have some place to be, even if it is in the same room, but with other people, especially if it is with other people! Especially if those other people are women! That works like a charm!

Getting a phone number has become much easier these days thanks to Facebook. So what I am going to show you now is a way to Facebook close, and also get a number. There are two ways to do this, the old fashioned way, with pen and paper (which means you have to have a pen on you, and a napkin somewhere very handy) or your cell phone, especially if you have a smart phone.

It is important that you get their information. Don't give them your phone number and expect them to call you. Women are too passive in nature to do that, and it makes you look like a Beta Male. Even though they will be chasing you by this point, you need to have the option to follow up. Getting contact information makes you look high value anyway, and raises the chances for future meetings, especially since you are the one in control of the situation.

The "Facebook" Close

First, let me say that handling multiple relationships on Facebook can be difficult. Everyone can see whom you are talking to (except on chat) when people tag you in photos and write on your wall. A good Alpha can leverage this stuff and actually use it to his advantage. A lot of people get in trouble on Facebook, so be careful. Facebook can be great, but tricky, territory.

When you are coming to the end of an encounter with a new person, the easiest way to get a lot of information is to say "we should be friends on Facebook." For some reason, even though Facebook exposes tons of personal information quickly, people are pretty likely to add you, right then and there, especially if you have proven to be high value. It is "safe," for most people, at least in their minds, and people love to add friends to their Facebook tribe. I don't always like the exposure that Facebook gives, and the more exposure you have, the less control you have over a situation.

That being said, most people are happy to add you on Facebook, especially if you have done things right. Becoming a Facebook friend can lead to getting other info as well.

Referring to Robert Cialdini's book, <u>Influence,</u> there is another "law" of influence called the "Law of Consistency." This law states that people like to be consistent and congruent in their actions. This is why the "agree" sets we discussed are so effective. The more you get someone to agree with you, the more likely they are to agree with you again! This is the essence of the "Law of Consistency."

So, to utilize this law with the close, you use the Facebook close to get other things. If you are using a piece of paper and pen, because you don't have a smart phone, you can still make this work. You should probably get a smart phone, because it makes a lot of things easier, but this works too. In order to get her Facebook profile, ask her to write down her email address, so you can look her up when you get home. She needs to write it, not you, and this is important.

Once you have gotten her to write, then she is likely to continue writing, according to the law of consistency. While she is writing her email address, simply say, "why don't you just put your number there too?" More than likely, she will simply just continue writing (since she already complied with your first request to write her email) and write her phone number. Bing! You now have her Facebook, email address, and phone number! I will tell you how to use those things in a bit.

If you have a smart phone, you can do something similar. Add her on Facebook right there in front of her. Ask her for her email, and put it into the Facebook application. If she has a smart phone, she will probably confirm you on the spot. Now you are "friends" for real; there is no "foe" in sight. Getting her number is a simple matter at this point, since she has already added you on Facebook, she is already, in a sense, compliant, so all you have to say, since you both have your phones out, is "what is your number? I will send you a text so you will have mine." Send the text. Now she has your number and you have hers!

Be cool and casual about it, as you have been about everything at this point, and end things by saying something indefinite like this: "We should hang out sometime." Don't ask her on a "date," but just to hang out. I think the whole idea of "dating" is crap anyway because it puts too much pressure on people to be disingenuous, and it puts her defenses up when you go on your "date," since you are probably trying to get something from her, at least in her mind. Hanging out is "safe" and ambiguous enough, so neither is sure if you are being friendly or romantic. We will cover "hanging out" in the next chapter.

Difficult Closes

You may find yourself in situations when a close is difficult. Lesson number one is to avoid difficult closes by closing early. Don't wait until the end of the night to close, or the end of a vacation, convention, etc., to get her number and contact information. You never know what may happen in the future that will complicate your plans. However, if you find yourself in a difficult close situation, all is not lost, although you will have to be more flexible.

On one vacation, a friend of ours was trying to close with three women (he was busy), and, after building rapport for a few days, none of them were around the last two days of the vacation. Not one! However, he wasn't going to be defeated because these women clearly adored me. In one case he left a business card with a girl's colleague, with a personalized note to her on back. For the other two, I found them on Facebook and sent them messages along with friend requests.

We generally advise against these methods. They did work, but they may or may not work for you. One of the reasons they worked is that he totally wowed these women during his interactions with them. He demonstrated my absolutely crazy high value to them, so the abnormal closes worked. If you impress them enough, and if you have adaptability, you can close even in less than ideal circumstances.

Besides demonstrating high value, these difficult closes worked for two other reasons. First, the business card worked because it contained a funny message related to a conversation our friend had with one of the girls. The message on the back of the card was personalized and showed high value. Do not just leave a card. Women are too passive to respond to that. Even with a message, many women won't respond, but a funny and relevant message increases the odds she will contact you. Second, he included high value messages with my Facebook requests. They were written in a way that said he was pretty much doing *them* a favor by requesting their friendship!

Following Up

The question that has plagued men around the world since the phone was invented has been: how long should I wait before I call her? Trick question! In this day-and-age you shouldn't call, not with Facebook, email, texting, homing pigeons, bat signals, etc.; there is no reason to call a girl anymore. Calling a girl opens up all sorts of awkwardness. If she doesn't recognize the number, she probably won't pick up, and then you have to leave a message. If you do call her and get voice mail, which you will, just leave a short message like: "hey, it's Joe, just calling to say hey!" Short and sweet, no rambling. If she does pick up, which she won't, then you need to have things to say right away. Back in the day, the phone was the only way to get a hold of a girl, other than walking up to her house, or secretly following her wherever she went! I have, of course, not done that since high school............... Anyway. With a variety of other means of communication available these days, phones are your last option. The traditional amount of time to wait after meeting a girl is three days.

Here is a hard and fast rule about when to follow up: follow up when you are detached. If you are nervous, anxious, or worried that you will screw things up, you probably will. Wait until you are calm and cool. If you are feeling this way about a girl you met, and really want to call her, call another female friend, one you are detached from, and just chat her up for a while. You can be excellent and detached when talking to her, then hang up, and follow up with your dream girl. If you never get to the point where you can be detached following up with her, then just throw her number out, de-friend her on Facebook, and move on with your life. No girl is worth losing your mind over.

In the modern age, I think a follow-up needs to happen a little faster than it used to, simply because there are a lot of distractions. Today, I think you need to follow-up within one or two days at the most. The follow up should be quick and non-threatening, and detached. We will go over some ways to do this so that you can build "virtual" rapport via the technology available to us today.

<u>Text Messages</u>

For girls, texting is like crack. They love getting them, and they love texting. So if you don't have an unlimited texting plan, get one, or go live in a cave. A text message follow-up should occur within 24 hours, especially if you didn't immediately see her put you into her phone when you got her number. Memories fade quickly, and even though you made a great impression, enough to get her number and follow up info, since you aren't verbally talking to her (so she remembers your voice), you need to keep things fresh in her mind.

That follow up text should look something like this:

"Hey, Joe here from last night - glad you got to meet me!"

This text is effective because it is confident and a little cocky. Hopefully you made a strong impression with her (i.e. you came across as confident and high value), because a text message like this looks a little weird coming from a shy beta male. We really haven't covered cocky in this book, at least not directly, but the teasing really falls under the idea of cocky humor. Women love cocky humor, which is why teasing works so well. Text messages should always be short, so avoid the novels. Long messages show attachment.

When she texts you back (and she will if you send her a cool and calm text like this one), don't respond immediately. Wait awhile. Remember, since you are excellent, you are a busy guy. Your responses should be brief, cocky, and humorous. If she likes you, she will initiate a conversation via text. They love having conversations via text. Just roll with it, but be the first to end it. You can end it one of two ways. Just don't respond, which is better, or say that you need to go because you have to do (whatever). Always have a reason to leave. You are a busy and valuable guy. Make it something good and valuable too.

You can and should propose that you hang out in your texts, typing something like "we should hang out sometime." Gauge her response, and if she says "yes," remind her of how busy you are. "I am pretty booked up this week, but I can make time for you Thursday afternoon, and we can grab coffee or something." See, you are making time for her in your "busy" schedule. Being "booked up" means whatever you need it to. Do this toward the end of your conversation, and, if you can, pair it together with the "I need to go" text, which will enact the law of scarcity.

When you meet her for coffee, you should arrive just a little late. Make her wait. She will start to think you are standing her up, and be relieved when you show up. Do all of the rapport building techniques we have covered, have some routines handy in case the conversation goes stale, and make sure you break rapport occasionally, so she chases you. Have a friend text you while you are there and take the text. Don't follow her around wherever she goes. In fact, you should walk away from her. Make sure you sit in a way so you can touch her, or she can touch you. This is not a book about how to go out on a date, but we will write that one soon, so please stay tuned.

For the purposes of this book, just know that dating is really an extension of that first meeting. The more time you spend with her, the more rapport you can build, and that is basically how relationships are formed. Don't forget to casually touch her like you would a friend, as good touching builds comfort. Always be the one to end your time together.

Facebook and Social Media

When it comes to using Facebook to follow up, a bit more subtlety is required. Don't ever, ever, "poke" a girl, unless you already know her well and you are using it as a kind of online flirting. That stuff is creepy. You can write on her wall similar to the first text mentioned above, or send her a message. Remember; make it brief, cocky and humorous. The Facebook follow-up will take a little longer. Building up to something on Facebook can take a couple of days of contact. Finally, you just need to say something like "we need to hang out sometime!" and play it by ear.

When following up, giving too much information on your part is death. Remain mysterious, but casual, and be cool and detached. Women can detect nervousness from a mile away, so if you need some practice, call a friend and chat with him or her before you send that first text or Facebook message.

Chapter Twenty-One: Building a Relationship and Sex

As we have continually stated, The Joe Alpha Factor is dedicated to helping you form good relationships that last for the long term. Friendships are just as important as romantic relationships, and a lot of what we have said even applies to business relationships, since humans are basically the same in any circumstance. Not only can you form those relationships, but you can conduct yourself in a way that permits everyone to get what they need out of the relationship.

Building a solid relationship takes time. Maintaining a relationship is a lot of work. Don't let anyone fool you. While we do believe in "casting your nets wide," (that is casually dating a few women at a time so as to avoid detachment) we are not proponents of a "love'em and leave'em" mentality

"Dating"

That being said, let's talk a little about "dating."

What a terrible, horrible, misinterpreted word "dating" is. It has caused the downfall of a ton of potentially good relationships in the last fifty years or so within modern Western culture. In my mind, "dating" is synonymous with a job interview, because that is what most dates are.

A date in modern Western culture is about two people sitting at a table, putting something into their gullets, and grilling each other. It is also about hiding your bad, or less than desirable qualities, and presenting your excellent qualities, in order to get the other person to like you enough to spend more time with you in the future. Except for the food component, that is the definition of a job interview! You go in, put your best foot forward, hide your undesirable qualities, so you can spend more time with the guy who is interviewing you, or, in other words, get the job. You are doing the same thing to the employer. You are sizing them up, to see if the job is a fit for you, and they will be presenting the company as a place with great benefits, good pay, and a good environment. You will not find out your boss is a jerk, or that you are expected to work weekends, until you have been working there awhile.

No one is completely honest in an interview. And no one is completely honest on a "date" either! I think dating is horrible, especially for guys. Despite women having jobs and being "liberated," there is still a cultural expectation that the man pays for everything. It isn't really even cultural, but it is a way to prove that a man can both provide and protect. He buys her food to show his value. I don't really have a problem with that part, since I buy food all the time for people I go out with. However, I don't do it because I want them to like me. I do it because I am an Alpha provider/protector. I have an innate sense of wanting to provide for my "tribe."

Beta Males pay for everything to bribe the girl into liking him. He reasons that if he buys her dinner, then she has to like him, or kiss him, or whatever else he thinks he is paying for. That attitude and frame will kill you in the end. The Alpha does it because it is the right thing to do, whether she likes him for it or not. Same activity, different frame of mind.

Still, if an Alpha is "casting his nets wide," he will be going on a lot of "dates." That gets expensive, if you follow the traditional date model of dinner, followed by an activity of some kind. I think that should be saved for later. We will get to that.

Everyone is defensive for the reasons I outlined above. It turns into an interview, and people get nervous and attached.

If you follow-up with a woman (sometimes you won't, simply because you'll lose interest, which happens when you have a lot of fish in your nets), never follow the "date" model. Before you use your resources to provide and protect them, they need to prove their worth to me! Talk about a switch up!

Hanging Out

Usually on the follow-up, I recommend that you "hang out." Hanging out creates a different mentality. It is casual and low pressure. It isn't a "date" when you think about having to hold her hand, or kiss her at the end. She has permission to pay for her own crap (although it is still good to do, as a show of Alpha value). "Hanging out" should not be dinner and a show. It should be coffee or drinks, something low key and inexpensive. If you have a mutual interest, then suggest doing that together, especially if the activity is inexpensive. Walk dogs together. If you do comfortable things, you will be comfortable. Comfort is where rapport is established and grown, and comfort is where relationships lie.

It is also less threatening to ask someone to hang out than it is to ask them on a date. It is really the same thing, but it is a re-frame of the activity to make it less threatening to everyone. While hanging out, everything we have already taught, body language, routines (to help establish the flow of normal conversation and save stale conversation), mirroring/pacing, etc., should be utilized. When you are hanging out for the first time you need to talk. Remember what we said about talking? Women want you to talk because it is a demonstration of value. As the relationship progresses, she will talk more. Don't worry; you don't have to do all the talking all the time. In fact, there are times when you should just shut your yapper.

When you go hang out, like for coffee, have a plan ready to do something after, like walk around a mall or go to a park. If the encounter goes well, use it. If it doesn't, bail. Always be ready, and always be in charge of the plans. We will talk about the "Alpha

Attitude" in the next chapter so you will learn how to always be the Alpha.

A Female Friend vs. a Girlfriend

We believe it is good to have female "friends" for a variety of reasons, because it is always good to expand your network of friends, and you can always meet potential romantic interests through female friends. Nonetheless, it is tricky, and there are positives and negatives to it. Most Beta Males secretly hate their female friends because they can't move out of the "friend zone."

The "Friend Zone"

If a girl says, "I just want to be friends," you are done. Absolutely done. When a girl uses those words, it is like a nuclear missile blowing up your city. It means you have not only lost her as a romantic interest, but it also usually means she doesn't even see you as a friend! I know that sounds weird, but if she uses words like "friend," "big brother," "pal," etc., all she sees you as is a Beta pushover. Once you are in the "Friend Zone," and she will let you know that you are there, all hopes for any kind of relationship is usually lost. Get out. Go to greener pastures. There are lots of other women out there. Once you are in the "Friend Zone," that is where you live in her mind. In my experience, it means that she isn't even attracted to you as a friend.

I have friends - good ones. They call me, and I call them. If a girl puts you into the "Friend Zone," she is not your "friend." It is a nice way of dumping you. If you think she really wants to be friends, then try an experiment. Don't call her. I guarantee she will never, ever call you. Friends call each other. The word "friend" is the worst thing a girl can say to a guy. Ever. Again, if she has to say it, then she is neither your friend, nor a potential romantic interest, no matter how hard you try to change the situation. If she *is* your friend, she will never have to say it. You will just act like friends, call, and hang out, with no pressure. I mean, how often do you have to declare that you are friends with your real friends? Probably never.

I haven't had a girl say we were "just friends" in 15 years, but I remember the one that did, and it still burns me to this day. Can you tell? It means you have been rejected. Forever. Okay, it is possible to get out of it, by the way, but the work involved is simply not worth it when you can start over with another girl. Why waste your time winning over a girl that doesn't want you when there are thousands out there willing to chase you?

Female Friends

I have dated a lot of girls, and had some great relationships that started out romantically, progressed romantically, and came to their natural end. Yet, the girls that I think about to this day, 10 to 15 years later, are the ones I was friends with first. Real friends. The friend relationships are relationships that *really* stick out in my mind.

That is not to say that you shouldn't have eventual romantic intentions in mind when you befriend a girl, but the most intense romantic relationships start out as friendships. Then, something suddenly flipped and they fall for you, or you for them, or both!!! It is pretty amazing really.

So, whenever you meet someone, build as much rapport as possible, hang out, spend and time with them, but my frame of mind is always "friends first." The reason is so that you are detached, excellent, and gone. You are never nervous around your friends and am my most authentic self around them. I am always excellent around my friends. I can touch my friends on the arm or shoulder, or even hug some of them, and it is natural, and not weird. I don't flip out when my friends leave. You need to develop this mindset with women. Go into a frame of "friendship first," because it tricks you into not having the anxiety that goes with dating. Women will find you irresistible.

It is more for your own mental state than for hers. If you have this mental state, your value always shines, since you are detached and excellent. If something happens, great! If something doesn't, then I have a friend! You will never ever disappointed.

Real female friends (not girls that have put you in the "Friend Zone") are some of the most valuable people to have in your life. You never have to say you are friends either, by the way. As I said above, if that ever has to be verbalized ("you are my friend," "let's just be friends," "you are like a big brother to me," etc.) that is the end of the relationship altogether.

Female friends can help you dress attractively, help you meet other women with ease, and help you pick out the good ones from the bad ones. Hell, your best nights out in the field will be nights that you hang out with female friends. This is due to the "Law of Social Proof," as outlined in Cialdini's book <u>Influence</u>. The "Law of Social Proof" basically states that if two or three people are doing something, then it must be acceptable to join in.

Here is a fun little test of that law that I tried last New Year's in Rome. Get together with two friends, and look upwards in the same direction. People will stop and look, just because you are!

So if you are with a girl already, that gives you "social proof," namely that you have value enough for a girl to want to hang out with you! It gives the other girls in the room notice that you are "pre-approved," i.e. you are excellent, or else that girl wouldn't be hanging out with you. Remember, "work the whole room," because people are watching you all the time, whether you know it or not! Sometimes they don't know they are watching you either, as the subconscious mind takes in a lot of information that we don't consciously process.

Funny things happen when you become real friends with a girl. A lot of the time, you have a great resource at your fingertips, and a great friendship. But other times, as I have mentioned, the switch flips and you have the best romantic relationship of your life. It is really something.

Watch the movie <u>When Harry Met Sally.</u> It is all in that movie. There is a reason that movie is still popular 20 years later. It is true: men and women ultimately cannot have a deep and meaningful relationship with each other and it not turn into something deeper. And usually it was the girl who changed the nature of the relationship, not the guy. Thus, there can be a real benefit in being real friends with women.

<u>Romantic Relationships</u>

Maybe you are just in the mood for an old fashioned romance. That is good too! They are a lot of fun and always exciting. The rules that we have outlined above apply. You have to show yourself as high value. You have to be confident, and you have to build rapport. The only major difference is the amount of touching. When you are in a romantic relationship, you will touch each other more than if you were just friends. You hold hands, you kiss, and you have sex.

In romantic relationships you should always be advancing. Always advancing means that you should progressively ramp up the amount of physical contact you have with a woman, at a pace that makes her comfortable. And the second that she shows discomfort, you back off, and go back to a level that she is comfortable with, and then advance again when comfort has been reestablished.

Never ever ever ever force a girl to do anything against her will.

That will land you in jail and is called sexual assault and/or rape. At the very least, it is a bad idea. Never make a girl uncomfortable, and if you do, simply back off, and let her come back to you. As long as she is attracted to you, she will.

Sex

"Sex is like pizza; when it is good, it is good. When it is bad, it is still pretty good." According to the Internet, this quote comes from either Mel Brooks or Sharon Stone. Either way, it pretty much describes the way most people view sex, doesn't it?

I think it was the comedian Jeff Foxworthy that said men are like fireworks, women are like steam engines. Fireworks take little effort to light and shoot off, whereas steam engines need primed, and warmed up in order to get hot. Women are just like that. You need to "prime" them in order to get physical with them. I don't care if it is your girlfriend, wife, or the girl at the nightclub you just met, they need primed and warmed up. Their sex drives are simply not as quick as ours to get going. Often, for women, sex is less about the activity and physical feeling, and more about being an emotional expression of the relationship.

I have a friend who says, regarding married couples, that "sex starts by doing the dishes." This means that for a woman, sex is based on valuable actions, relationships, and long term "priming."

It has been said that women need to be in love to have sex, and men need sex to fall in love. That isn't really the case all the time, but it is a general rule you can follow. Remember, women had a lot to lose if they mated with the wrong guy back in the jungle. She had to ensure the guy was going to stick around to take care of the kids, and a relationship built on all the things we have talked about thus far made it more certain that he was going to stick around. Remember this though: women like sex as much as men, but for different reasons!

Sex is a complex thing. This book is really not going to cover it, but a couple of things are important to mention. Sex will never ever happen without comfort. If someone, especially the woman, is uncomfortable, it won't happen. Never force a girl, drug a girl, get a girl so drunk that she can't make decisions, and have sex with her. It needs to be something you both choose to do.

Sex is a very personal thing for everyone, including you, because you have to make yourself emotionally and physically vulnerable to have sex

Sex is an organic process. You don't just meet a girl and have sex. You have to do all the things we have mentioned. You have to build rapport and trust, verbally, physically, etc. While it is possible to get a girl to go home with you at a club, I have found that you simply need to be detached from that, and have plenty of fish in your nets. If you do things right, have the right mindset, and connect with her on several levels, sex will just naturally happen. Sex is a good thing. We wouldn't be here without it!

Remember, "there are no victims, just volunteers." Make sure that everyone you have sex with wants to be in that situation. Remind them of this if they get mad that you have other "fish" in your nets.

I have my own moral code regarding sex, and you have yours. We make no judgments in this book about those moral codes; we are simply teaching techniques on how to build relationships with women, and how to develop a mindset for being attractive. Use what you have learned here responsibly, and never to hurt someone.

Chapter Twenty-Two: Attitude

Being an Alpha Male is 90% attitude. Your attitude will determine your understanding of your value, which will in turn determine your body language, your voice tonality, what you say, your confidence level, and most importantly, how others see you. There is a particular frame of mind that you have to have to be an Alpha Male. It isn't based on looks, or position (but usually people with "position" are Alpha Males, at least in that environment), but it has to do with how you frame the world, yourself, and others.

Most of what we believe and know comes from other people. This book is a mix of two things, our own personal experiences, as well as research. Not all of these ideas come from our experience (however a lot does) but much of it has come from research that has been confirmed by experience. So when it comes down to it, what you know about most things comes from an outside source.

Let me give you an example. What is going on in Iraq these days? Who is running for president? You only know the answers to these questions because someone told you the answers. That means that "they" told you about things the way they perceived those events, and in the way "they" wanted you to perceive these events. You could go to Iraq and find out how things really are, but most of the time we are at the mercy of other peoples' "frames."

"Frames" are the way that we see things, the lens through which we make heads and tails of reality. We can't take in every bit of information, so we have to delete (choose what we don't say or share) generalize (simplify and categorize), and make sense of information the best way we can. Some of that information comes from our experience, but a lot of it comes from outside of ourselves.

There is nothing wrong with listening to other people. You have been listening to The Joe Alpha Factor frames for the last couple hundred pages or so. It is a frame of mind that has helped us meet people in the past. You have your frame of mind, which a mix of your own perceptions, and what other people have told you. Don't just take our word for what we have to say though - go out and try it. Tailor it to yourself, and see if it works.

See, this is where people get into trouble: they accept frames and perceptions from other sources as gospel truth. For example, people watch the news and assume they know a presidential candidate because Fox News or CNN (who have radically different frames of mind from each other) have reported on him. In reality, it is not the "facts" that are being reported, but facts that are delivered along with a particular frame. Many people don't question those frames, frames which are, especially in regards to the media, skewed. They do not tell you the "truth," but rather their version of it. For example, they may delete information that makes a candidate look good, or generalize that all Republicans hold to a certain position, when it is not true.

It is not just media outlets that impose their frames upon us. Our families do it. Our culture does it. Schools do it. You probably spent at least twelve years, if not more, sitting in a classroom being told what to think and how to think.

I am not saying that the frames of other people aren't helpful. Cultures exist because cultural frames are helpful. Schools are supposed to help us learn useful tools so we can function successfully in society, like how to read and write. Encountering the frames of other people, and even buying into them, are not bad. We hope you are buying into the frame of mind of this book! Here is the problem: blind adherence and acceptance of frames without question. "Blind faith," in other words.

Some realities have to be accepted on blind faith. The human brain has evolved to operate efficiently, and part of this means that we aren't equipped to verify every fact independently. I am not going to go to Iraq and see how things really are. I will analyze all the frames of the competing news networks, assume that their frames skew the truth in one direction or another, compare them, and get a general sense of how things are. I have no desire to investigate every grocery item I buy to make sure there are no misprints on the label.

However, some frames need questioned, especially social or cultural frames of mind that may be limiting our ability to succeed and thrive. I hope we have challenged some of your frames about women, men, and nature. We provide you these frames because we hope that a change will help you to get what you want: a relationship, and in particular, a relationship with the woman of your dreams.

In short, this is the attitude an Alpha Male must take. He is a guy who encounters the world, encounters various frames of mind, and challenges those frames of mind with his experience and learning (an Alpha Male is always learning by the way). After challenging frames, he then frames his reality in the way that HE wants.

One of our most helpful sayings is "he who controls the frame, controls the game." In other words, if you can get everyone else to see your frame of reality, you will be in charge. Let me give you an example. You are late for work. When you arrive, you say nothing, and your boss sees you and pulls you into his office and rips you for being late. Your boss set the frame. However, can you imagine walking in late and telling your boss "traffic was horrible today, and there was a big wreck, but thanks to some defensive driving, instead of getting here an hour late, I am only ten minutes behind? I am glad I got my reports done last night!" What reasonable boss would rip you in this instance? Do you see the difference? In the latter case, YOU set the frame, instead of letting your boss set it.

Again, we are not saying reject all outside frames of mind. Obviously, your boss is right, in the sense that it is best to arrive to work on time. So, if you rejected *all* outside frames, you would have to make up your own language, because language itself is a frame of mind. What we are saying is to take the information from your experience, as well as from outside sources, and establish a frame of mind that is helpful to you. In the end, the Alpha Male is not the passive man who simply accepts what he is told on blind faith. The Alpha Male *creates the frames that other people accept.*

This is the key to being an Alpha Male. The real essential difference between being and Alpha, Beta, Gamma or whatever is your frame of mind, i.e. your attitude. The Alpha Male creates the person he wants to be, whereas other men take the lazy way out and let others set their reality for them. Taken to an extreme, this can lead to a victim mentality, a "woe is me" attitude where everything is somebody else's fault; an Alpha Male is not a victim.

Every frame you encounter should be challenged to the best of your ability. Accept the ones that match up with experience, and reject the ones that do not. Even better, take it all into account and create your own frame. CNN and Fox News do it, and millions blindly follow. Why can't you do the same? We have created our frames, and we found followers too. We control the frame. We control the game which is life. We always say "if you aren't in charge, somebody else is." Somebody out there is controlling the frame. That "someone" might as well be you!

We have a goal at The Joe Alpha Factor, and that is to train guys so they don't need our frames anymore, and they can create their own. In Herman Hesse's novel <u>Siddhartha</u>, Siddhartha had to let his son leave his home, and experience the world on his own. A good Alpha Male wants the same for other Alpha Males. We *want* our clients to leave us, and form their own tribes, and, of course, to be the chiefs of those tribes. Does this mean we might be making our own competition? Yes, but we can handle it.

Challenging Some Shaky Frames

For the last part of this chapter we are going to examine some common Western cultural frames, related to meeting women and forming relationships. There are many accepted cultural frames that are downright erroneous and unhelpful when it comes to meeting and maintaining relationships with women.

Women Should be Placed on a Pedestal

Biologically, women are more valuable than men, as we covered earlier in this book. One egg a month, one baby a year, versus a man who produces millions of sperm a day, and can have lots of kids, as long as he has willing partners. There is a biological reason we say "women and children first," when there is an emergency. Further, fairy tales and movies have bombarded us with the tale of the damsel in distress, and the prince risking his life to save her, like Helen of Troy who was pretty enough to start a 20-year war.

Don't get me wrong, I love women. I think they are great. I have lots of women in my life, and they are fun and confusing, and wonderful and frustrating all at the same time! But, one of the things this culture has done is to put women on an absurdly high pedestal. They are not better, or worse, than men. They are different, very different, and biologically more valuable when it comes to egg and sperm, but women are not more, or less special than men. They are just *homo sapiens*, like us, trying to survive and procreate. Men and women are ultimately equal. Don't let feminists or misogynist men (men that hate women), or the guys that fall all over women worshiping them, tell you otherwise.

The reason I am saying this is simple: if you put women on a pedestal, you will never be able to talk to one. They will always elude your grasp, as if they are living in an ivory tower. There is nothing mysterious about them, or powerful, to the extent that you need to be nervous, shaky, or awkward around them. They are people. If you approach women while remembering that they are just people, you will be more detached, calm, and able to be excellent.

That being said, they do have wonderful things to offer us men. Get to know them for their complementary differences, enjoy being confused by them, but don't put them on a pedestal where they are so out of reach that even the thought of approaching them fills you with terror. For all you ladies reading this, know that I love you. I am trying to help good men meet you, which they will never do if they are afraid of you!

The nice thing about teasing is that is knocks women off their pedestals, and brings them a little closer to earth. They need that. They don't want people to worship them and kiss their butt. If they did, then Beta Males would rule the earth, and have dates, and we all know this isn't true. You will find that women, like men, are fairly consistent in their behavior nature, which is why our techniques work. Once you shift frames to enjoy the great things women have to offer, instead of putting them out of reach, you will have fun getting to know them. In the end, women want to be treated normally.

Women Know What They Want

Ask a woman what type of guy she is interested. They have a list. They always have a list in their heads, and I promise you, you are probably not on that list. No one is. It is a list based entirely in fantasy. The list usually describes a guy that is tall, dark, handsome, rich, successful, sensitive, and slightly edgy, but only when she wants him to be. Women have to have that list in their head to have some kind of standard by which to judge men.

The same fairy tales that told us that women are in some ivory tower waiting to be rescued have also taught women that there is some perfect Prince Charming out there waiting for them. Women have the perfect guy envisioned in their mind, and if you try to be that perfect guy, you will be destroyed. This is what Beta Males do, by the way, and it doesn't work. They try to be the perfect guy that meets these wild and unrealistic expectations.

That being said, women will ditch that whole list that they have concocted (or been given, by hours of watching Disney princesses) for a man of high value. I know women that say they want tall muscular men with dark hair, yet have married short, doughy, bald guys! Have you ever seen a big guy, or an ugly guy, with a super-pretty girl? This happens all the time, and if you asked that girl what she wanted before she met him, I bet you dollars to donuts that he would not fit that description.

There is a real difference between what women want by nature (which we have covered) and what the culture, friends, media, movies, magazines, etc., tell women what they should want. What women ultimately want is a high value, confident man, who can connect with her emotionally, mentally, and physically - a man who is not afraid of her, and does not put her on some silly pedestal where she is out of reach. She also doesn't want a guy that worships her or tries to bribe her. Unless she is a narcissist, she isn't attracted to guys with such needy and passive attitudes. Heck, I would argue that even narcissists ultimately want a valuable man.

Looks Matter to Women

This leads us to another bad frame. Okay, nobody is attracted to ugly people. I get that, but looks matter way more to men than they do to women. I have seen plenty of super good looking, hunky dudes, with big muscles and great hair, strike out repeatedly with women. Since I am at my core flexible, I roll with the punches. I am an Alpha Male, not because of how I look, but because of who I am, and the frame of mind that I maintain.

There is a time and a place when looks matter a little more to women, and that is in those fertile times of the month. During this time, studies have shown that women tend to be more attracted to physical features than personality, simply because their biology is telling them that good looking, healthy men, produce good looking, and healthy children. That biological bias is fairly easy to overcome. That being said, who would you rather be in the forest with? The good looking guy with no confidence, or the guy who can out think the lion? So while you should be concerned with looking healthy (see below; this is more important to a woman than looking "good,"), confidence and value are the key.

Remember why this is: women are looking for confident men, to provide and protect, and offer safety and security. A man does not have to be handsome to do this, but he has to be confident. So a man can be handsome, but lack confidence, and he will be as alone as the ugly girl. Men look for reproductive value, so physically attractive women, who are expressing signs of fertility and health, are going to have the advantage. Despite the educational system and talk show hosts telling us otherwise, I am sorry ladies that happen to be reading this book, it is true. All the "awareness" in the world can't rewire hundreds of thousands of years of evolutionary wiring.

Looks matter more to men than they do women in the long run. Women may deny this, but our experience states otherwise. Women generally think long-term when it comes to mating (provide and protect, safety and survival) whereas men tend to thing shorter term (how fast can I get my genetic material out there?!).

Before I close this section, I must note a few things about looks. First, as I have mentioned, men need to look "put together," i.e. look classy based on their situation in life. Unless you are a rock musician, you should look neat, clean, and taken care of. Women may not base attraction on your natural looks, but they do pay attention to your appearance.

Don't look like a slob or weirdo. Plus, as we have mentioned, the more put-together you look, the more confident you will seem. Second, some evidence suggests that people are attracted to others with strong immune systems. This is because a healthy immune system ensures survival, a fact especially true before the discovery of antibiotics and modern medicine. Looking, and actually being, healthy may give you an edge over the unhealthy guy. So, get some sleep, exercise, and watch what you eat.

Types Not, Leagues

This brings us to a very important frame that everyone needs to get past. Any time I hear a guy say "she is out of my league," I want to shock him with a taser. Seriously. I never do, of course, but I want to. This is an example of "high horse," or pedestal thinking. A lot of the time, what "league" a woman is in is based on how good looking she is, and how unattractive the man in question is. However, as we have mentioned many times, looks don't matter that much.

We have a principle called "types, not leagues." What we mean is that we tend to be attracted to particular types of people (body types, personality types, economic or social status, girls with problems, tall girls, short women, assertive women, passive women etc.).

In the end, while you may be attracted to a certain "type," there is no such thing as a woman who is "out of your league." Any man can be attractive to any woman he wants to attract. While women also have types they prefer, a man can override this preference by being a man of high value. Women will abandon their preferred types for a high value man. It happens, and you can make it happen for you if you are high value enough.

I still have a surprised reaction when I see an ugly man and a beautiful girl, sometimes. A few weeks ago I saw this stunningly beautiful woman with this short fat man that looked like an Ewok. She was clearly madly in love with the guy. I thought to myself "what the hell?!" Then I remembered how things work. Even I still have to combat unhelpful or untrue frames of mind sometimes.

There is no such thing as a "league" when it comes to women. Just because the movies tell us that certain women are "out of your league" or that all women are only attracted to chiseled, Hollywood leading men, doesn't mean it is true. Remember, any man can make himself attractive to any woman if he can establish and maintain the mental frame of being an attractive, high value, Alpha Male. And, the first place that frame exists, is his own mind.

Women Want a "Nice Guy"

Nope. Definitely N-O-T!

I am sure that your dad, step-dad, or even a sitcom dad said that in order to win a woman's heart, you must be super nice, buy her flowers, and tell her how much you love her. You need to buy her dinners, presents, and gifts, compliment her, and help her move furniture. And, women themselves have probably told you this too. They whine and whine about their jerk boyfriends to you while complaining there are no nice guys out there! "But," you tell yourself, "I am nice! Why won't she date me?" That is because you know, and so does she, that when all is said and done, she isn't really attracted to nice guys.

Basically, friends, teachers, relatives, and society in general tell us that in order to attract a woman you have to be extra nice and passive, i.e. you have to put her on that pedestal. Whatever brother or friend or TV show or book you got that from, it is hogwash. This is not to say you shouldn't do nice things for the women in your life, but you have to do them with the right frame of mind. Do them because they are the right thing to do, not because you are trying to bribe her or force her to like you. Many men are doormats, thinking that if they are just nice enough, buy them enough stuff, or express their feelings, or whatever other bribe they can conjure up, she will fall madly in love with him.

This isn't really even true in movies! Watch a romantic comedy sometime. When you get a girlfriend, you may have to watch a few of them. They are rigidly formulaic. The guy is always edgy, and a bit of an jerk. He is assertive. He is confident. He remains that way through the whole movie, until the end, when whatever craptastic writer wrote the movie flips everything on its head and he chases her through an airport/train station/crowded room. That is when the movie ends, usually. The strong confident character trades it all in to chase after the girl he has fallen for.

There is a reason the movie has to end there. When he started to chase her, the dude gave up all the things that attracted the girl to him in the first place: his confidence, self-respect, value, detachment, and flexibility. The movie *has* to end here, because if we really got to see what happens after the credits, the girl would get tired of that butt kissing bull-crap and leave him.

Romantic movies get it half-right. Well, even mostly right, up until the end at least, when the dude betrays his very nature and becomes a Beta Male. He starts out as an excellent and high value Alpha Male, and is a totally different guy by the end. No wonder women think they want nice guys, and guys try to be nice guys, because that is what the mainstream media is telling us will lead to "Happily Ever After." However, as most "nice guys" like you know, this doesn't work.

Real life tends to be different. Women tend to date two kinds of men. Gamma Males, the jerks whose aggressiveness is often confused with assertive confidence, and confident Alpha Males, who make up about 10% of the general population. The remaining females get stuck with varying levels of Beta Males, and have to live in unhappy marriages.

Obviously, we are not saying you should become an aggressive jerk, and we are not saying to be mean to these women, like a Gamma, but we are saying don't be a wimp, a butt kisser, or a sycophant. Women are absolutely repulsed by these types of men! I am too frankly. But in the culture we are in, a lot of women get railroaded into unhappy marriages with men that either are Beta Males, or become Beta later in the relationship.

So yeah, be a little edgy, and always be confident and assertive. If they test your confidence, hold your ground. Don't give into everything. Don't bribe them into liking you. Be a man of quality and value and she *will* be attracted to you. If she isn't, be detached and let her walk away. She won't walk if you are a detached and high-quality Alpha Male. And if you are a detached and high-quality Alpha Male, your intrinsic value won't come from the validation of some female, but the knowledge of your own interior excellence. If a girl is too dumb or short-sighted to see your value, and ends up walking away, it is her loss. You will have plenty of fish in your nets if you are an Alpha Male.

So yea, do good stuff for people, say good things to them if they are true, and appropriate, but do it because it is the right thing to do or say, and not to just kiss anyone's butt. Also, an Alpha Male speaks up when he sees something wrong. He points out things when they are crap. He is confident enough to speak the truth whenever and wherever because it is the right thing to do at that moment (note: don't be a complaining, whiny, Beta Male; speaking the truth when necessary is different than constantly whining!). If they walk away from you because you are valuable and confident enough to speak the truth, then it is their loss not yours. In short, be a man, and you will be attractive to everyone.

Why Marriages and Relationships Fail

This brings us to why relationships fail. In an online lecture, Dr. Robert Sapolsky of the California Academy of Science compared humans to other primates. He pointed out that one trait that differentiates humans from other primates is that male humans are much more likely to completely submit to their female mates! Amazing, and true, too.

This is one reason why marriages fail. The man becomes completely submissive (Beta) to his wife! He stops being a man! Romantic comedies are correct here too. However, it doesn't happen as quickly as a two hour movie might have us believe. Women are always going to be attracted to high value men. That doesn't change. I have seen Alpha Males marry the most beautiful women in the world, and years later be shells of themselves because they have chased her around, trying to please her. Once you compromise your value to bribe someone into liking you, it is a sign of the end. Neither the man nor the woman will be happy in this scenario.

So even in marriage, or long term relationships, a man must be concerned with his value above all else. You should not put up with a woman who emasculates you. If a woman walks out the door, and she won't if you are a high value male (she just won't - I promise), don't run after her. You are detached, excellent and gone in every circumstance. You can be flexible (we will cover that more extensively in the last chapter), and compromise with people, but you should never, ever, ever, trade in your dignity just to get someone to like you, even if that person is your wife or girlfriend.

There was a great movie, well, actually it is a really hard movie to watch, that came out in 2010, called Blue Valentine. Watch it. Memorize it. It turned my stomach. It chronicles a couple at the beginning and end of their relationship. The girl gets pregnant from a Gamma Male, she finds a good man who is an Alpha, who later turns Beta as the relationship progresses. There is a part where he *begs* her to have sex with him. It is sickening. It literally upset my stomach to watch. I can't imagine living like that.

It is this transition to "Betadom" that ultimately makes the woman disgusted with her husband, and the marriage end with him just sort of walking away, no house, no money, and his spirit crushed. I can't tell you how many times I have encountered this scenario, in which wives find other men because their husbands have Beta-ed their way out of their hearts.

If you find yourself compromising your dignity, or losing your confidence, just to get attention from a woman (we are describing the "Moby Dick" scenario from earlier in the book) it is better to lose the woman than your dignity. I promise though, you won't lose her if you don't compromise your Alpha Male frame of mind. If your wife respects you, if you are excellent, if your worth is not attached to her approval, you will never lose her. It is the greatest paradox in the universe!

Chapter Twenty-Three: AMOG: The Tribal Leader

Tribalism explains how all of this comes together. Long before we were humans, we were hanging out in tribes, and our essential wiring is tribal in nature. As individualistic as this culture seems to be, we cannot get away from the tribal way of thinking. The ones that seem to shake off tribalism spend their time in the basement playing video games by themselves at best, and, at worst, live in shacks thinking of ways to blow people up. We call these lone wolves "Omega Males," by the way. Watch the movie <u>The Hangover</u>, and it is easy to pick out the Omega (hint, he is the guy with the beard). While you are at it, pick out the Alpha, the Beta, and even the Gamma in that movie!

So what is an Alpha Male really? He is the guy that becomes the leader of the tribe. The leader of the pack. He is the guy who creates the frame of mind for others to follow. He creates rapport through empathy, confidence, detachment, flexibility, and value. If he doesn't have a particular skill, he influences the guy that has it. He takes risks, and, unlike the Gamma or the Beta, watches out for the good of the whole tribe.

There are two ways to become an Alpha Male. The bulk of this book is about that: how to enter a tribe and become the Alpha Male. First, Alpha Males enter into the tribe, and learn how to become the one that influences the thoughts and actions of the whole tribe.

Basically, you enter a preexisting tribe and become its leader. Wherever I go, I become the Alpha Male of every tribe I enter, because I know how to effectively build relationships with different tribes. There isn't a tribe I can't enter. Rarely do I enter a tribe and not become the most influential person in the tribe. The head of the tribe is the guy that women want to be with.

The second way to become an Alpha Male is to form your own tribe. Either way, the process is the same: you build relationships with people around you, and become the one who sets the frame of mind.

The Alpha Male of the Group (AMOG) does not influence by force, but by charisma. He attracts, but does not push. He communicates his sense of value, and people follow. If they don't follow, he lets them go and find their own way, and welcomes them back if they fail.

An AMOG is the leader of a particular group (or set) of people that you may encounter. People hang out in groups, and those groups usually have a leader. The AMOG is that leader. You need to identify the AMOG of the tribe you are attempting to enter. Sometimes, the leader of a particular group is a Gamma Male, by the way, and he leads them by force, not charisma. There is a difference.

Winning Over the Whole Group

At The Joe Alpha Factor, AMOG takes on a slightly different tone. We believe you still want to become the AMOG, the most influential person in the group, but you want to do it by winning over the whole group, including the current dude in charge.

Whenever you enter a group of people, there will be obstacles, i.e. people who automatically put you into the "foe" category, rather than identifying you as a friend. Remember, that is the default setting. So if you want to talk to a girl in a given group, you really have to win over the whole group for that to work. This includes the men and the women.

Remember, you catch more flies with honey than vinegar, so if you approach the entire group and win them over, you not only get a relationship with a new woman, but you now have other friends that will help you, watch your back, and establish your value as an Alpha Male.

One of the things that I have learned is to never piss off the AMOG. If the AMOG is a Gamma, he is ticked anyway, but you can even win him over. Some Gammas cannot be won. There is nothing wrong with walking away from a drunk angry Gamma who is threatened by you. I use the same techniques on the men, Alphas and Gammas, as I do with the women, since it all works the same way. You want to get men and women to like you, not by bribery, but by being a quality guy.

When you meet a Gamma, just be the better man. Don't fight him if he wants to fight. Win him over too. If you can't, walk away. Betas will be threatened by you as well, but they are passive-aggressive, and won't really be that much of an initial threat. They will become your Betas soon enough anyway, if they see the women take an interest in you. That is because they will do anything to please women, which means after you win over the women with them, they will start to suck up to you!

If you meet a group with a true Alpha, don't try to outgun him. Get him on your side and become the Alpha to him. While this book is primarily about meeting women, Alpha Males are much more than that: they are leaders of men. If you win the group over, and become the tribal chief through charisma and value, I guarantee you will have more women attracted to you than you can handle!

My business partners and I have noticed this over the years: true Alphas respect other Alphas. An Alpha Male is cool with another Alpha. It is the Gammas and the Betas that you will have a harder time with, because they are naturally and innately insecure. Other Alphas won't be threatened by you, and will actually help you, if it is in the best interest of their "tribe." Alphas, in the truest sense, should be working together. Collaboration is a quality of the Alpha Male, as long as it does not pose a threat to their tribe or its members. In other words, if you meet a group of people with an Alpha Male, win him over, become his friend, and the whole group will follow suit.

An Interesting and Rare Example

We had a graduate of our program that moved to another state. He increased his general level of confidence, and applied for a great job, and, with his new-found confidence, got it. Don't forget, our program helps you to create the reality you want, not just with women, but in your career and other areas. He got settled into his job, started making friends in the city, going on dates, forming his tribe, etc.

Along the way, he made friends with a lot of people, and among them was a couple. Both were good-looking and smart, but not married. She was cute as a button. Our former client became friends them both, won both the guy and the girl over, and made them part of his "tribe." Soon, it was clear that the girl was attracted to our client, and they started "hanging out," and eventually some sparks began to fly. We had created this guy to be a very high value man. Here is the thing: the guy knew she was hanging out with our client. He knew that sparks were flying, and there was even some physical stuff going on, and he remained loyal to our client, even after our client essentially "stole" his girlfriend.

Now we are not going to say this will happen all the time, and we don't recommend that you steal girlfriends, fiancées, wives, etc. from other dudes (even though it is stupidly easy to do if you are a high value male. Trust me, rings don't mean much these days, even to a woman), but this is a case in which becoming the tribal leader gave our client access to just about anything he wanted, and he even kept the loyalty of his newly found Beta Male. Everyone loves a high value man. Women want to be with him, men want to be him, and if they can't, they are content with basking in the Alpha Male glow, and simply following him.

You will always have "competition" for women. You have two choices in dealing with competitors. Win them like you win the women, and become their Alpha, or fight them to the death because you will tick them off. Frankly, no girl is worth fighting over, so I prefer just to become the leader of the whole tribe. The "Law of Liking" and the "Law of Authority" (as found in Robert Cialdini's book) are more powerful than you think.

By the way, the same is true for "obstacles" when you meet women. Obstacles are other women who are going to try and block you from talking to the girl you are interested in. You have experienced it before. You approach a girl, she seems interested, and her mean friend pretty much ends it either by her words and actions, or just her negative body language. These women do it because they might be uglier than their friends, in a bad mood, or even jealous that you are talking to their friend instead of them. Whatever crazy reason they might conjure up, they are trying to block you, so *win them over too*. Always remember to focus on winning the group, and if you do that, you will win the girl, and gain some followers to watch your back in the future.

Rites of Passage

As you enter into a new tribe, except one you started, you will have to prove yourself. There will be tests and rites of passage to endure. This is proof of your mettle, and your value. You can't just walk in and become the AMOG. You have to draw people to yourself, and prove that you are the real deal.

In regards to this, there are formal rites of passage. In a fraternity, we call it hazing. In the military we call it boot camp. Churches call it confirmation; Jews call it Bar mitzvah. Every culture has rites of passage that prove the worthiness of men. African tribes go on hunts; some others have painful tests of stamina. You will encounter those in the tribes you enter as well. Some from the men, but mostly from the women.

We are not going to go over the rites of passage when you enter groups of other men. As I mentioned, if you are going to the army, joining a fraternity, becoming a Mason, or whatever, there are rituals and requirements to prove your manliness to the other men. In the movie 300, King Leonidas has to kill the wolf before he can join Spartan society. This is a universal law in every culture for a boy to become a man. In our other books we will cover how to be the Alpha in a group of men, how to past the ritual tests, and become successful in every environment.

Women Will Test You

Women have rites of passage that they will force you to go through. Remember, women, like a group of men, are looking for the highest value and the most excellent man they can get. The better the man, the higher the chances of survival and the better babies they can make.

These rites of passage that a woman puts every potential suitor through are hard wired into their brains. They have to do this. When we were running around the forests and jungles, the women that tested their men survived and reproduced, and the ones that didn't were killed because they mated with a weak Beta, or an apathetic Gamma.

These "tests" are an unconscious (and frankly, sometimes conscious) attempt to see if you really are the confident, detached, and flexible man that you portend to be. Sometimes they are small, sometimes they are huge. But you need to learn to recognize these tests when you are entering into the tribe, so you can pass them. The whole tribe will be watching how you perform on these tests. The rites of passage from men are easy to see and overcome, but the ones from women are like stealth bombers.

These tests continue through life. Even in marriage, I have seen women testing the mettle of their husbands. The ones that fail get left for higher value men, if the women are still attractive enough to have options.

When you first meet a girl, as we have covered previously, the first test might be simply that she will ignore you and see how you handle it. Maybe she will ask you to buy her a drink. (Beta Males always oblige, of course, to bribe her into liking them). Maybe she will mention she has a boyfriend. Perhaps she will make fun of you, criticize your clothing or physical appearance. She might call you gay, weird, or too old for her. She may mention that she is too religious to "date" or that she is too busy to talk to you. "Tests" come in all shapes and sizes, and women throw them out all the time.

It is right that they do this, for the evolutionary reasons that we have outlined many times. If they pick a bad mate, they are screwed. That wiring is still present in their brains. How do you pass these tests then? Be a man. Be an Alpha. In other words, be confident, funny, flexible, detached, and unshaken. If she has closed off body language and won't talk to you, talk to her friends instead. If she asks you to buy her a drink, tell her to buy you one. If she makes fun of you, tease the heck out of her (which you should be doing anyway). Teasing is the equivalent "tests" that men give to women. If she says she has a boyfriend, ask his name, and start talking about him in a positive way. If his name comes out quickly, she really does have a boyfriend. If not, she is lying, and you can tease her about that. Either way, boyfriend or no boyfriend, it doesn't matter; you can still win her over.

Most Beta Males will respond to their tests in a variety of wrong ways. Some respond with extreme disappointment, shown in their words and body language. Some will get angry and visibly frustrated at the girl for being taken (as if it is a big deal - it isn't). Other Betas will just freeze right there, looking very awkward. Notice, based on our suggested responses at the end of this chapter, that the Alpha Male just rolls with her tests, makes light of them, and remains just as confident after the tests as he did before.

Again, let me repeat. *You cannot get bothered by their tests - at all.* You have to roll with them, continuing to be the high value man that you always are (this includes your body language). A few weeks ago, my buddy and his brother were talking to some 21 year olds in line to get into a college club. One of the girls said we were "weird" (her other friend was into us by the way). He made a few comments, ignored her, and entered the bar. They had to visit the bathroom, which was occupied, and sure enough, guess who was waiting by it? Yep. That girl. Being forced to stand near her, my friend didn't get angry or bothered, and continued to be confident and funny, even calling her on the "gigantic emotional brick wall" that separated her from knowing him (and gesturing about its size for added fun). Let's just say that my friend and his brother talked to her, and her many friends that came and went, for the next hour. She basically proclaimed her boyfriend a Beta Male that needs our services, and she added our friend on Google+ later. I think our friend passed her tests, don't you? It's actually easy to pass, if you know what women are doing with them.

If you are married or dating, and your significant other is upset at you, and won't tell you what it is about, just walk away. Don't ever chase a woman, no matter what her relationship is to you. Make them chase you! Empathy and emotional connection are fine, as long as it is not done in a Beta, i.e., needy, way. Despite what women may occasionally claim, they, like all people, hate needy men.

Here is the thing guys: the tests go on forever. They will always be testing your Alpha mettle. If you fail enough, they will find a higher value man than you. Never, ever compromise yourself, your integrity, your confidence, or your value to pass a test from a woman. That, in and of itself, passes the test. You will fail a few times. You will fail a lot, frankly, but remember to recover, move on, and pass the next one. There is no failure, just feedback. After a while, you will start to see the tests for what they are. I have found that they start to go away the more you pass them. But of course, that makes them harder to detect, and they will never entirely disappear.

This is all part of the game. We are wired like this because it has helped us survive and pass down superior genes from one generation to the next. I suspect women will eventually read this book, and that is cool. Please get upset and declare vehemently that you never do this, and then go out and ask a guy to move your dresser into your new apartment, and call him your "buddy" when it is all done. That is a test too.

Below I provide a few sample shit tests, along with the Beta (wrong) response, and a good Alpha Male response that is confident, flexible, charming and funny.

"Are You Gay?"
    Alpha: Yes, I am very happy, thanks for asking
    Beta: Silence with a sad expression

"Aren't you a little short for me?"
    Alpha: Yes, I am short, but very awesome
    Beta: Silence with a sad expression

"I can't talk to you. I have a boyfriend"
    Alpha: That's okay, I have a girlfriend. Maybe we should introduce them to each other
    Beta: Oh okay, sorry to waste your time

"Why don't you buy me a beer?"
Alpha: You're in luck! I know the supplier here; I'll place an order, and in 2 weeks your drink will arrive.
Beta: Sure! Be right back...don't go anywhere

"I don't think I like you"
    Alpha: You're right; you don't like me, you love me
    Beta: Sorry about that

I have to give props to Weezer for the idea for that last one, as it was inspired by a lyric from their song "I am the Greatest Man Who Ever Lived" a good Alpha Male song if there ever was one.

Chapter Twenty-Four: Conclusion

It is challenging to write a book like this. Not because we struggle to fill the pages, but because there is so much more we would like to say. If you have made it this far, you realize that there are so many more applications to our techniques that go far beyond meeting women and forming relationships with them. We at The Joe Alpha Factor are students of human nature, both from our own experience, and by looking to the frames of mind of others. It is amazing to watch our clients grow into a way of thinking by which they can get anything they want out of life, without the specter of failure hanging over their heads, since failure is really not part of our own frame of mind.

So, we have left a lot of things out that will go into other books, or that you can learn from us through consultation. Always be sure to check out joealpha.com, and sign up for our newsletter. Keep an eye out for our new books. We have books on being popular (geared toward younger people), and how to be a celebrity. We have gathered materials, research, and experiences that will help you to get a job, attract money, fame, power, and people into your life, and how to deal with disappointments and setbacks. In short, the same basic techniques that allow you to be successful with women can be used to make you successful in everything you do.

As we briefly mentioned in this book, being an Alpha Male is something that you can learn to do. While some people are born with a tendency toward Alpha traits, anybody can become more (or less, in the case of many married guys) of an Alpha Male. It can really be boiled down to a series of techniques that utilize the basic consistency of human nature, along with some confident thinking and helpful frames of mind.

However, there is another level: the Theta Male. He is the enlightened Alpha. He is not an Alpha because of technique, but because he has a deep understanding of how the universe works, and how to influence it. Theta Males have a type of spirituality that is also practical, one that understands relationships, not on a merely human level, but at a fundamental level of universal reality. This is truly exciting stuff, but not available in a book, or available to the masses. We are not starting a secret society, but simply stating that not everybody is able to - or wants to - be a Theta Male. However, if we find a guy that can and will be a Theta Male, we will gladly tell him how to become one.

That being said, there is one last thing that is the hallmark of the Alpha Male: flexibility. It is something that has been hinted at and even mentioned throughout the book. The person with the most flexibility in a given system has the most influence in that system. He is the guy that can enter into the frames of another person, or of a group or tribe, pace and mirror that, and then lead them into a new frame of mind.

Have you ever met rigid people? People that only see things their way? Perhaps at times they have fought their way to power, but often, then are just disliked by others, and are extremely unhappy people. The people that can go with the flow, without losing their identity and still maintain influence over their environment, are the guys that are happy, powerful, and bring happiness to the people around them. They realize that everyone is different, and by being flexible, they are responsible for foraging a path to happiness in this life.

So roll with the punches. Whenever a situation arises, be flexible enough to find the most helpful strategy to reach your desired outcome. If this girl doesn't work out, there are a lot more. If this job interview doesn't get you a job, go on another. If you aren't making money in one field, pursue something different. Flexibility is linked to detachment, i.e. not being anxious about outcomes, which we have shared extensively in this book.

In the end, a lot of people do things that are not helpful because they are not flexible. They learned to do things one way, and that is what they know, and, helpful or not, they are unwilling or incapable of changing their internal (mental) and external (actions) strategies, even if their current strategies aren't working. They are incapable of entering into another person's frame of mind. They lack empathy, awareness of themselves and others, and they lack effectiveness.

So, flexibility is really a mental construct. It is the ability to discard what is not working to achieve a particular end, and finding strategies that work to achieve that end. The Alpha Male will always be a flexible leader. Flexibility leads to confidence and achievement.

Humans are the most naturally flexible creatures that have roamed the earth. I remember watching a <u>National Geographic</u> special about evolution. Imagine that, huh?! Anyway, there were two competing sets of hominids (pre-humans). One ate bugs and the other ate whatever they could find. The first was very successful and the second had troubles because of what appeared to be a lack of consistency in their diet. They were always trying new things, and the others just stuck with their bugs.

Once the climate changed, and the bugs died off, guess who made it. The ones who were flexible. The bug eaters would only eat bugs. The bugs died, and so did they. Inflexibility, i.e. rigidity, killed them forever, and the other group eventually became us.

Being an Alpha Male is more than just attracting women. I hope we have made this point abundantly clear. Being an Alpha Male is about protecting the tribe. It is about standing up to danger and difficulty. It is being your own man. It is about being a leader. Being a kiss butt or a lone wolf is not going to get the job done.

Look at a guy like Donald Trump. Read one of his books sometime. He is fiercely loyal to people and they are fiercely loyal to him. That is why he is successful. He has no problem marrying supermodels and I bet women throw themselves at him all the time. An Alpha Male has a state of mind that affects everything he touches. Women are easy to attract (as is money, fame, fortune, etc.) if you are an Alpha.

If you would like to keep up with us, be trained by us (we are net savvy and can meet with you on Skype or other platforms if you are outside our geographical reach), or just receive email tips and notifications about our products, be sure to go to www.JoeAlpha.com and sign up for the newsletter. Do it now. The book isn't going anywhere!

We hope that the principles in this book have challenged and shaped your own frames. However, we have just provided you with a jumping off point; you have to go out and do the work. Practice meeting people, anyone. Treat everyone the same. Joke around and help people, because it is the right thing to do, not to get them to like you. Be someone that people want to follow, and they will follow. If they don't want to follow you, then be detached and flexible, and let them go. Don't ever waste your time on someone, a girl, a boss, a friend- no one- who doesn't actively want to spend time with you.

Joe Alpha Edition Bonus Chapter One:

<u>Four Social Media Mistakes You Are Making Right Now And How To Fix Them</u>

If you haven't thought much about how you act on social media, now is the time to face up to the reality that what you do on Facebook, Twitter, and other social media is very important. People spend a lot of time on these sites, and guess what? What you do on social media sites will influence people's opinions of you for a long time. In fact, with the new Facebook timeline, everything you have said or done will be available to the ages.

When you use Facebook and other social media sites, everything you say and do is right there, wide open, for your entire online social world to see – and judge. Just as in the "real world," women (and friends, co-workers, and potential employers) are subconsciously and consciously analyzing your updates, photos, and comments, and putting you in a variety of zones. These include the dreaded "creeper zone" and "friend zone" but also the "romantic zone," if you play your cards right.

In this chapter, I will list four social media mistakes you could be making, that keep you squarely in the "friend zone," and prevent you from getting a date. I will also explain why they are mistakes and how to fix them. This is not an exhaustive lists of mistakes, but it is a good start.

Mistake One: You Play Too Many Facebook Games

Women want a confident and able man that can protect and provide. Evolution has wired this desire into their brains. They know intuitively that if you spend your day raising virtual crops, feeding virtual pets, and developing your alter ego as a knight, then you probably aren't going to provide for her needs in the real world. Even females that play online games probably want a guy that doesn't play a lot of online games. Yes, it is strange, but women look for different qualities in men they are attracted to, than they do with friends, and your goal, I am sure, is to get out of that friend zone.

The solution is to either not play so many online games, or at least clear your Facebook wall of the posts about them. I know that you can meet women through games, and some guys have done it this way. However, if you do meet women like this, be sure to clearly demonstrate that while you enjoy playing online games, you also have other activities in your life.

Mistake Two: You Whine Too Much

"Thank you! Spend all night chatting with me at the bar and then leave with your jerk of a boyfriend!"

A friend of mine posted a status update just like this. I changed the exact wording to protect the dateless. This is whining. He is not just whining privately, but in front of hundreds of online friends.

Frustration is a normal emotion, and I agree that his situation was frustrating. However, venting online like this is a bad idea. Vent to your friends in private, not to your entire online social network. This status says he is angry, passive, desperate, and bitter, which are not qualities women love in men! A confident man would have blown the whole incident off, or, said something to the girl at that time if he was frustrated with her.

This particular update also shows that my friend's value was too low to ultimately win over this girl. In other words, anyone reading this got the impression he was not a high value guy.

The simplest solution is to not post stuff like this. Don't post things that make you look like a complainer or whiner. Another solution is to take a bad situation and re-frame it, since YOU control what you post. It is likely that nobody from his social network, save a friend or two, was at that bar that night. So, instead of posting something whiny, he could have posted about how much fun he had, and how great it was to meet so many new people. This would have made him seem confident and attractive, instead of coming across as a loser.

Mistake Three: You are Online Too Much

Think of successful people. Pro athletes, famous musicians, business executives, etc. Are they online all day making random status updates, sharing goofy pictures, and commenting anytime somebody posts something? No way. They are successful and busy. If you are on Facebook or Twitter all day, it tells people that you don't have much of a life. You don't want your friends and co-workers to know you as "that guy they have to block from their feeds" because you don't have a life. Remember: excellent guys are busy being excellent.

The solution to this problem is twofold. First, get a hobby. Become good at doing something. Take classes. Learn how to earn money. Practice a sport. Write a book. Do something excellent that requires time on your part. Second, stop being online so often, and explain to your social group, indirectly, why this is so. For example, you might make occasional updates about being busy lately attending business conferences, which suggests you are starting your own business. You could mention a 5K you are training for, or finishing the first chapter of your new book. Now, you think of something!

Robert Cialdini, in his book <u>Influence</u>, explains the scarcity principle, which is that the less something is available, the more people are likely to value it. So, the lesson is, become more scarce, and people will perceive you as more valuable, as opposed to being the expendable guy that has so much free time he can hang out on Facebook all day.

Mistake Four: You Suck-Up To Your Female Friends Too Much

A relative of mine is always complaining about how bad her life is, and how horrible her ex-husband is. Yes he is a jerk, and so were her first two husbands. She can really choose winners, that's for sure. So, the result is that her Facebook feed is filled with drama, with plenty of women gladly wading into the conversation giving her plenty of "hell yeahs!" and "you're rights!" However, most guys don't want to get involved in that conversation, except the occasional Beta Male that jumps in to agree with her, in an attempt to impress her.

They do this, and guess what? They are in the friend zone immediately. How do I know? Because unfortunately, my relative wouldn't date a guy that agrees with her. So far, she hasn't attracted one yet that does.

I have another Facebook buddy that thinks he will get a date by kissing up to women, so he always posts about loving the "Twilight" books or he rants about how he can't stand jerks that mistreat women. Maybe he does like "Twilight" and I certainly agree with him that jerks are bad news, but his posts always come across as trying too hard to impress women. And most women see beyond it anyway. They classify him into two categories: a Beta Male kiss-up who is trying to win them over romantically by agreeing with them, or as a good friend. I know him, and trust me, he wants a relationship, not another "good female friend."

The solution to this mistake is simple. First, don't agree with women all the time on social media (or in real life – but that is beyond the scope of this chapter!). Take a risk and disagree with them. You may even want to call them out occasionally (be funny and charming about it, of course). The "risk" is that you may be de-friended, but by disagreeing with them, you will definitely crawl out of the friend zone.

A friend of mine, let's call her Beth, always posts about her drama with her boyfriend. They are "on again" and "off again." During one of their "on again" moments, she posted about loving her "baby boy." I couldn't resist, so I responded that I didn't know she had a baby, and I asked if he was teething yet. I got a playful, pretend angry response. When she is "off again" and posting about her relationship woes, a long list of Beta Males show up to offer to talk to her and help her, whereas I either ignore the drama, or if I do occasionally respond, it is to playfully tease her about it. Not surprisingly, the Beta Males never get a response, but you can bet that I do.

Second, don't post something just to kiss up. If you really love "Twilight" then (it is even painful to type this…) post about it. However, if you are doing it solely to impress a girl, then stop yourself. Remember, your goal is to impress a woman by being detached, excellent, and funny, not by trying to impress her by acting like a woman. From reading this book, you should have gathered by now that acting like a woman is *not* how you get a date with one.

In conclusion, remember social media allows you to broadcast yourself to the world. It is hard to make your past "go away" online, so you want to be just as much of an Alpha Male online as you are offline. So, stop making these four mistakes, and guess what? You will start becoming more attractive to your female friends, and your friends and co-workers may actually enjoy reading your updates instead of blocking them.

Joe Alpha Edition Bonus Chapter Two:

Six Quick Tips To Meet Women At The Gym

Many guys go to the gym regularly to make themselves look more physically attractive, and to feel better physically and emotionally. They also find themselves surrounded by lots of lovely ladies, and naturally want to meet some of them. So how do you do this?

Well, we know the stereotypes: gyms are meat markets, fit guys get women with ease, etc. However, in reality, the gym is just like any other setting in life: the Alphas (the excellent, detached, confident guys) get the women, while the Beta Males (shy, lacking in confidence) don't.

Before I give some tips, I want to make a quick point: women don't value looks in men as much as men value them in women. It is great that you are sculpting your body, but don't forget that most of the work you should be doing to meet women is mental in nature. In other words, having the biggest muscles, being able to run ten miles on the treadmill, or possessing abs of steel aren't guarantees of success with women. Every gym has its less fit Alpha Males who get the ladies, and its Beta males who are in top shape, but lonely.

The gym is a tough place to meet women. Sure, there are a lot of them around (and a lot of them are in great shape), but there are other big disadvantages. First, gyms are often loud places and it's hard to work your game. Not only that, but most women wear headphones, which makes initiating a conversation difficult. And, women perceive gyms as meat markets, so they're often on their next to highest guard (after clubs). However, here are tips that will help you meet women at the gym:

One: Be Excellent

Alpha Males are always excellent in all their environments. So, if you're at a gym, you should be excellent there. This means the usual confidence, detachment, extroversion, etc. However, it also means you should be in decent shape and be able to hold your own. You don't have to be LeBron James or be able to run a marathon, but you can't look like a wimp when lifting weights or let a cardio machine own you. If you need to work out a little at home first, then do it. I've had great success with Beachbody's Insanity and Asylum. They're intense and easy to do at home.

Two: Have Impeccable Body Language

You must have confident body language. Keep your head up. Walk, run, and exercise like you own the place. Imagine you own the gym and everybody loves you and admires you. Next, ask yourself, "how would I act in this situation?" Now, act just like that!

That is how you have confident body language. When I run at the gym, I make sure I run in a confident way. My head is up and I am pretty relaxed. I make sure people know that when I run, I am just as in charge as when I am walking or sitting.

Three: Be Detached

Guys at the gym typically do one of two things: they either outright hit on women without end, or stare at them. Both can be creepy. In both cases, they can show you care a little too much and are not very high value. Women like guys that are detached. If you are the only one not staring at them, or hitting on them, you'll stick out in a good way. Ignore them. In fact, be a little cocky about your ignoring them. They will be shocked that YOU could ignore THEM, and they will want to earn your attention.

Once they see that you don't care too much, you can casually strike up a conversation, but only as an afterthought. It seems odd, but it works. However, be sure to ignore them out of excellence, not fear. And, they can tell the difference.

Four: Have a Life Outside of the Gym

Women can tell the guys who spend all day at the gym. And, that means you seem like you have no life outside of fitness. While being in shape is an indicator of excellence, if that's all you have, you're basically a loser. Walk in the gym in a suit and tie, take a business call occasionally, and take a couple of days off from the place (you can still work out at home). Don't let them think your only life is at a place where people come to get sweaty and leave.

Five: Know What Women Really Value

Women don't like biceps. They don't like goatees. They don't care that you can squat five more pounds if you grunt. Oh, and they sure as hell don't think weight belts are sexy.

When it comes to looks, studies have shown that women prefer fit, but generally average guys. They like the All-American guy. It doesn't mean you have to stop getting big and lifting weights. However, just don't think all your efforts impressing your guy friends is going to impress the ladies. If you want the biggest biceps in the gym, then do it because you want to, because it likely isn't going to impress a woman. Go for that fit and athletic look, but don't look too bulky (from hitting the weights too hard) or too anorexic (from running hours and hours). And, remember, you must work your mental game.

Six: Approach With Care

Approaching women is another topic we've addressed in this book extensively. Remember that approaching at the gym is much more difficult due to noise, headphones, highly guarded attitudes, and even the fact that many women are there just to workout. Even though a man may always be on the prowl for a date, most women aren't actively looking (it goes back to their generally passive nature). Keep this in mind when you approach. Look for Signs of Attraction, like if she is looking over at you, flicking her hair, smiling, etc. If you see these, make eye contact and smile back. If she is free or casually working out, then you must say something, even if it's just hello. If she still has her headphones on, leave it at a smile. If she's interested, her headphones will come off. That is your sign to say something.

Another good tip is to approach women in places in the gym other than the workout area. This means the lobby, the pool, the hot tub, sauna, etc. Women are more open to interaction in these places because the expectation is more social.

See, you *can* meet women at the gym!

Bibliography and Suggested Reading

Cialdini, Robert B. Influence: The Psychology of Persuasion. New York, NY: Collins, 2007.

Driver, Janine, and Mariska Van. Aalst. You Say More than You Think. New York: Crown, 2010.

Fehmi, Les, and Jim Robbins. The Open-Focus Brain: Harnessing the Power of Attention to Heal Mind and Body. Boston: Trumpeter, 2007

Garner, Alan. Conversationally Speaking. Los Angeles: Lowell House, 1997.

Hawkins, David R. Power vs. Force: the Hidden Determinants of Human Behavior. Carlsbad, CA: Hay House, 2002.

Lieberman, David J. Get Anyone to Do Anything and Never Feel Powerless Again: Psychological Secrets to Predict, Control, and Influence Every Situation. New York: St. Martin's, 2000.

Navarro, Joe, and Marvin Karlins. What Every Body Is Saying: an Ex-FBI Agent's Guide to Speed-reading People. New York, NY: Collins Living, 2008.

Pease, Allan, and Barbara Pease. The Definitive Book of Body Language. New York: Bantam, 2006.

Pease, Allan, and Barbara Pease. Why Men Don't Listen and Women Can't Read Maps. New York: Broadway, 2001.

Ramachandran, V. S. The Tell-tale Brain: a Neuroscientist's Quest for What Makes Us Human. New York: W.W. Norton, 2011.

Schwartz, Jeffrey, and Rebecca Gladding. You Are Not Your Brain. New York: Avery, 2011.

www.ingramcontent.com/pod-product-compliance
Lightning Source LLC
Chambersburg PA
CBHW060821050426
42453CB00008B/531